Contents

If you want your book to compete in the marketplace, get some help publishing your book. Choose your assistants wisely so that you invest your time and money well.

If you have something to say, then prepare it, write it, and share it with the audience you have right now. Who knows? Another book might be waiting just around the corner.

You are … a unique human being,
and if you've got something to say,
say it,
and think well of yourself while
you're learning to say it better.
—David Mamet[1]

1   David Mamet, *True and False: Heresy and Common Sense for the Actor (University of Michigan: Pantheon Books, 1997)*, 51.

CHAPTER 1

How to Write a Great Book

The way you write a great book is to prepare a great book. Following the proven steps in this book will make the process more efficient and more enjoyable for you, and your end product will be an exceptional experience for your readers.

Writing a book can be simple, but it's not easy. From concept to a book ready to share with others, there are potential hang-ups along the way that can make the writing and publishing process challenging.

The good news is that writing a book can be easier than you think, and much, *much* easier than many people make it out to be. That's what this book is about—making it as easy as possible for you to prepare, write, and share your message.

Just writing a book usually won't get you far. Writing a *great* book and *building a platform* to share that book will get you much further much faster.

The way you *write* a great book is to *prepare* a great book. That's why two-thirds of this book is about preparing your thoughts and content before you actually start to write. I've seen authors save from $500 to $4,500 in editing fees by taking this approach.

I've worked with two people who wrote their books under the power of inspiration (without a specific plan) and it turned out well. Others have paid thousands of dollars to fix their manuscripts because they were merely a *head*, *heart*, or *hands* dump onto paper.

Don't think this can't be you. These authors are excellent leaders and communicators, but when it came to writing a book, their *information*, *passion*, or *action* put into writing needed focus and organization before an audience would follow past the first chapter.

I've written this book to help you avoid that path.

The Path to Write a Great Book

This book provides a clear path to writing a great book that you'll enjoy writing and that your readers can benefit from and enjoy.

Chapters 1–6 are full of perspective, encouragement, and many practical tips that will make the process easier, more efficient, and more enjoyable from start to end.

Chapters 7–12 take you through specific steps to create the structure for your book. You plan out other important projects and events in your life—weddings, meetings, vacations, building a house or a business, to-do lists to plan your day. Don't you think your book deserves and needs a good, solid plan?

Chapters 13–14 show you how to write and edit your book. Yes, it only takes two chapters to show you how to write a book. But it takes twelve chapters to help you shape your book to be a *great* book.

Chapters 15–17 show you three ways to share your book with others: finding a publisher, doing it yourself, or getting some help for a few essential parts that can potentially make or break your book.

I've also included a number of appendices as a reference guide to certain processes I explain in detail in the main chapters.

This book is a step-by-step guide—one that you can have open beside you as you sit down to accomplish your dream of writing a book.

My primary goal for this book isn't to help you find something to write about. Hopefully you already have a message within you. My goal is to help you *get the work done*—to get your message out in a manner that is clear, passionate, and purposeful.

(If you do need some help finding or narrowing the topic for your book, sign up for my five-day e-course at www.david-sluka.com/get-updates. Day 1 will help you find the right topic for you.)

Each chapter in this book is as short as it can be. The purpose of all I share with you is to:

- Help you think rightly about yourself as an author.
- Take a proven approach to the book-writing process, making it as efficient and enjoyable as possible.
- Accomplish specific steps so that by this time next year (hopefully much sooner) you will be sharing your book with others.

At the end of each chapter you will find "Your Assignment," which is a summary of the actions you need to take in response to the chapter. If you do each one, by the end of this book, you will have your book completed and ready to share with others.

If you follow my instructions, you'll get your book done well in less time with less effort and cost. So let's get busy getting your book written and have a blast in the process.

Your Assignment

1. If you're serious about writing a great book, consider how you're going to share your book when it's completed. I highly recommend the book *Platform* by Michael Hyatt, which will give you step-by-step instructions for building a platform.[1] If

---

1   www.michaelhyatt.com/platform.

you want to publish with a traditional publisher, having a significant audience who knows who you are and is ready to read your book is mandatory. But for anyone trying to build a platform, no matter the size, that book is full of practical steps, real-world examples, and helpful resources.

2. If you are still trying to figure out how you want to publish—find a traditional publisher or self-publish—I recommend that you skip ahead and read chapters 15–17 before going further. Those chapters may help you decide what path you want to take, which will affect your approach to writing your book.

3. If you have already started to write your book, please pause for now and reengage in writing your book when directed to do so in these chapters.

4. Get ready to write your book! Turn the page, read the chapter, and complete "Your Assignment" at the end. Then repeat for each chapter until this book and your book are done.

CHAPTER 2

Anyone Can Write

Among many voices speaking today, yours has its place.
Using reliable tools, you can write a book that others will want to read.

Shortly after one of my clients self-published her book, she received an e-mail from a past acquaintance containing the following unsolicited critique and advice—justifying it with her extensive and credible experience in the writing field:

> I found the book to be full of errors, not just grammatically, but it is also riddled with many elementary clichés along with irrelevant details that should not be in the book as they distract from the story. You jump around from thought to thought, event to event, without any transition, which leaves the reader confused. I only tell you this because if you are going to re-publish, you should hire a professional editor (not family or friends) or start over with a ghostwriter. There is no shame in not being a writer, but a non-writer should not attempt to self-publish a book without professional help.

She then said not to take her critique personally and that she was trying to be helpful. She finished by saying that she loved the title because "it starts out right away with intrigue and a hook."

These comments hit my client pretty hard, so she wrote to me, asking for my professional opinion. The following was my response to this author about her "friend":

> I completely disagree with her assessment and her point of view. Your book is not full of errors (you had it professionally proofread) and your story is well told. Her opinion is not helpful nor is it encouraging in any way, even if her credentials are valid. The only good she has to say about your book is that she likes the title?
>
> While there are ways any book can be improved, in no way do you need to start over with a ghostwriter. I'm not sure why she says you are not a writer, and I'm not sure what qualifies a person to be one in her opinion. You have told your story … in writing … which to me makes you a writer. Do you write full time for a living? No. But you have successfully written your story as an author.
>
> Please know that I believe in you and what you have written. This person is looking at how *she* would have written the book, not how *you* chose to tell *your* story. I'm shocked at how un-life-giving her comments were.

Anyone looking for hope will find it in your book. This woman was not looking for hope, so she didn't find it and only got tripped up in her rules of writing.

The author was encouraged by my point of view and thanked me for my support. The moral of the story is …

If you're a first-time author:

- Share your story. It's powerful. It should be heard.
- Present your message in the best possible way.
- Get input from trusted friends, and professionals if possible.
- Prepare for unsolicited comments that may not be all that helpful. Listen, but filter wisely.
- One benefit of self-publishing and print on demand is the ability to make changes because you don't have thousands of copies printed and distributed. If you discover that something isn't quite right, make changes for the next version.
- Celebrate because what you have written gives others access to the same hope, power, knowledge, wisdom, etc., you have experienced.

If you're a friend of a first-time author:

- Buy your friend's book. Don't expect a free copy. Also ask him or her to sign it for you.
- This person has just written tens of thousands of words over months, perhaps years. Find something good to say. As many things as possible.
- If it's a good book that you can honestly recommend, tell others about it through social media or whatever means you have.
- Share your critique only if asked. This can be tough, especially if you have editing or communication superpowers.
- If asked to provide input, choose your words wisely and provide *specific* examples so the author has clear direction about how to make his or her writing better.

A wise person can glean from any kind of critique, even if the feedback could have been presented better. But if you have nothing good to say, maybe you're just not the audience for that book. So then it's more about you than about the other person or the book itself.

I believe that those who have something to say should say it … as best as they can … and then share it with others.

Anyone Can Write

I love the movie *Ratatouille* (rat-a-TOO'-ee)—a story about a rat that dreams of becoming a world-class chef. The problem is that Remy is a rat, and rats and kitchens usually aren't a desirable combination. But Remy is inspired by the famous French chef Auguste Gusteau, whose motto is "Anyone can cook." The movie is about Remy's journey to show patrons of Gusteau's French restaurant and a very critical food critic that *anyone* can cook—even a rat.

I believe the same can be said about writing. Anyone can write. Whatever odds you are facing (thankfully you're not a rat), I want to encourage you that you *can* write a book. Maybe you won't be what some call a writer. But you can be an *author*. If you have something to share, you *should* write a book. A *great* book! That's what this book will help you to do.

Three Tragedies in Communication

I think there are three tragedies in communication:

- Someone who makes a lot of noise but has nothing to say.
- Someone who has something to say but says it poorly.
- Someone who has something to say but doesn't say it.

The last one is the most tragic. I can turn off what I don't want to listen to. But it's much harder to turn on what someone is keeping on the inside. This book is my effort to draw out what you have on the inside for others to experience.

Within a person who has something to say reside words of great wisdom, stability, power, and influence—often unknown to that person but still just as real. I personally am jealous to learn from a person like this. If I have the chance to have lunch with a person like this, I usually ask some good questions, then shut up and listen.

I once had a dream in which a person was on stage trying to speak to an audience, but the wireless microphone had no battery and the speaker could not be heard. In the dream I went to the sound booth, got some batteries, walked to the platform, put the batteries in the microphone, and handed the microphone back to the speaker so the audience could clearly hear what the speaker was saying.

This dream perfectly describes my ultimate purpose: *to help your voice be heard*. Practically speaking, that means helping you to take your message from wherever it is to its fullest expression.

Don't Add. Multiply. Ten Benefits of Writing a Book

Books are an amazing medium of communication. You can write your thoughts down on paper one time, and millions of people can read the same content at the same time, any time of day, without your needing to be present or do any additional work. Books utilize the power of multiplication.

Many leaders are in addition mode. Addition means that you have to be somewhere or do some kind of work for your message to spread. Addition means a lot of repetitive action in order to see significant growth.

Multiplication takes a different approach. You communicate something well one time in a medium that can be multiplied (like a book, video, or audio). Then others can review what you said as many times as needed without your needing to be present. When others learn about what you said and want to hear it too, on their own and without your knowledge they can access your content, read it, enjoy it, process it, learn from it, review it, practice it, teach it to others ... all without your knowledge or input. You've simply written and shared your content in a medium that supports multiplication.

See your book as an amazing way to multiply yourself and your message and affect people you cannot touch personally. With a book you'll be able to:

1. Document your expertise or experience *once*. You don't have to repeat yourself unless you want to.

2. Receive rewards (including residual income) as long as people continue to read your book, even though you've only written it once.

3. Give others access to your information at any time. While you're sleeping, a person anywhere in the world with access to the Internet can order, download, and read your book.

4. Teach more slowly. Others can take what you have to say at their own pace for maximum understanding and application.

5. Expand your influence. Help more people without having to be present.

6. Say your content better, clearer, with greater focus and organization. Writing a book formalizes your content. By *formalizes*, I mean that when you see what you have to say on paper, the gaps often become more evident than if it was only in your head or if you're speaking your message. Writing things down forces you to get your thoughts in order and makes them super clear if they're not.

7. Raise the quality of how you present the information after you've written the book. The book will bring out the best content you can offer, which you can make a part of any presentation you do after the book.

8. Establish your credibility. Having a book raises your personal and professional credibility in others' eyes.

9. Leave an important part of who you are to those who come after you. It's ridiculous to think that the human race has to continue making the same stupid mistakes generation after generation. Thank God for those who learn from others and go higher and further because they're standing on the shoulders of those who've gone before. Your book can be the foundation that others stand on to go higher.

10. Open more doors, like speaking engagements, business opportunities, consulting, interviews, and additional books.

For these and other reasons, I encourage you to step out of addition and into multiplication through writing a book.

First-Time Authors

Most of the first-time authors I work with are leaders who have shared their messages for years but have not yet taken the time to write down in book form what has so strongly encouraged others over the years. If you fall into this category, I'm excited to be with you on your journey. You are one of those I would gladly take out to lunch, ask questions, and enjoy listening to and learning from. (Your food will get cold, though, while you talk and I listen. Sorry about that.)

I also love working with people who don't have a large platform, yet their message is clear and they have a fire to share it. No matter who you are or what your writing experience, you can write a book that will inform and inspire others.

If you don't know what you want to write about, this book is not for you ... yet. Determine your topic first and then come back to this book. But if you do know what you want to write about and the message is one that has been burning in you for years, it's time to say it and share it in book form.

But There are *So* Many Books on the Market

One of my favorite places to visit is a bookstore. It's often the site of a date with my wife. I know, super romantic, right? But she likes it. Really.

Even though I've been writing professionally since 1990, it can still be overwhelming to walk into a large bookstore and see the voluminous supply of books on display. A Barnes and Noble bookstore in the USA can carry between sixty thousand and two hundred thousand books.

In writing this book I've run across talented experts who have many more years of experience and greater knowledge than what I could ever hope to capture in this book. To be honest, I've had my days of thinking, *This is depressing. What do I have to offer here with my little book?* Maybe you've thought the same thing about the book you want to write.

Let's look at some unnerving statistics:[1]

- In 2010 Google estimated that about 130 million unique book titles have been published since the world began publishing books.
- About three million new titles were published in 2011, and that number has grown each year since.
- About 15 million ISBNs (International Standard Book Numbers) were released in 2012.

---

1   Steve Spillman, "Author Tips: Facts You Need to Know," from Weekly Author Tips, September 11, 2013, weekly e-mail distribution, www.truepotentialmedia.com.

- As of September 2013, Amazon has about 22.5 million paperbacks, 8.3 million hardcovers, 1.1 million Kindle e-books, and forty thousand audio books available.
- With the flood of books on the market, most books sell fewer than five hundred copies.[1]

A number of years ago I walked into a bookstore and had an experience that changed my point of view about my place in this world. Like I usually do, I started looking at the new releases and books on topics of interest. But this time, instead of feeling intimidated and overwhelmed that I was in the pee-wees compared to these major-league writers, I had an impression that these best-selling authors were saying to me, "Come and stand with us—shoulder to shoulder. Say what you have to say. Make your contribution and walk with us."

I realized that what made what I had to say worthwhile wasn't having completely unique content that no one else could duplicate or say better. What would make my book special is that it would be from the one-of-a-kind me and would be my contribution to the world that some—not all—would appreciate and learn from.

The reason you should write a book is the same reason you have kids: because they're yours and no one else's. You will never hear a couple say, "We shouldn't have kids because our neighbors already have them. And look at how well they're raising them. We could never compete with that." Your children contain your unique image and influence, and they will carry on what you know and have experienced in this world. A book does the same thing.

I honestly think that the majority of people should write a book. Some people should be quiet, take a time out, and gather their thoughts for a while first. However, I believe that most people should share their life's learnings and experiences with others.

Maybe only your family and a few friends will read your book. Maybe it will be a best seller. Regardless, what you have to say should be said and heard.

What's Getting in the Way of Writing Your Book?

I've found that two things get in the way of people starting and completing a book:

- Time
- Trusted guidance to make sure they're on the right track

If you'll give me some time, I'll give you the guidance you need to prepare, write, and share your book.

---

1   Steve Spillman, "Author Tips: Join the Conversation," from Weekly Author Tips, September 19, 2013, weekly e-mail distribution, www.truepotentialmedia.com.

There's a great opportunity waiting for you. Many, many people are writing and publishing. Be one of them. Stand your ground; write a great book. Contribute to the world what is uniquely you, and do what it takes to get your voice heard by an audience waiting to hear from you.

Anyone can write. *You* can write. It's time to share what you have to say.

Your Assignment

1. Realize you have something to say. There's no one who can say it like you, and it's time to say it.

2. Read the article "Write Your Profitable Book Now! Don't Believe the Myths!" by Judy Cullins.[2]

3. If you were to give your book a title right now, what would it be? On a piece of paper or in an electronic document (like in Word, Pages, or Google Docs), jot down the topic you want to write about in a few words, in the form of a creative book title. If you have more than one book you want to write, choose the topic you're most passionate about or the one you want to write about first. If you have a few titles you're considering for your book, type those out so you can see them side-by-side.

4. Print out the piece of paper with your working title(s) and put it up in a prominent place where you will see it every day.

---

2   www.publishingbasics.com/2012/12/18/write-your-profitable-book-now-dont-believe-the-myths/.

CHAPTER 3

Questions to Ask Before You Begin

*Knowing the answers to these nine questions will help your voice
to be heard by the right audience with clarity, passion, and purpose.*

A dear friend and client was seventy years old when she set out to write her autobiography. Nine years later she had written only one page. Then she sat down with me, we worked together in the way I will work with you in this book, and a year later she had written and self-published an amazing autobiography with more than 130,000 words on 466 pages. The nine-year delay in writing her book wasn't because she didn't have anything to say. She clearly had a lot to say (and still has a lot to say)! She just didn't have a map and a plan to get the work done.

All that to say … please don't read this book in one sitting, hoping your book will get done because now you know more. Do what I ask you to do as I'm asking you to do it.

If you're serious about writing your book, go to your computer right now. Open a word-processing document. Read the rest of this chapter and then do Your Assignment. Then, for the next three days, read one chapter a day and do its assignment, which will take you to Step 1: Prepare.

If you haven't done Your Assignment from the end of chapters 1–2, please do those now before moving on. They will take less than a few minutes.

I'll wait for you.

* * * * *

Nine Questions

Let's get started with nine questions to ask yourself before you start writing your book. Write the answers to these questions in a word-processing document.

You may think some of the questions do not apply to you. For example, let's say you're writing your memoirs just to share with your family and you don't want to sell it to anyone else. If we were having lunch together, I'd ask you, "Why do you think that what you've learned and accomplished in your life would be of interest only to your family? Couldn't others benefit from hearing your story?"

So try to answer all of the questions, expanding your vision about who may want to read your book and the impact it could have.

This exercise will help you focus your thoughts about yourself, your message, your audience, and how you will reach that audience. A side benefit of doing this exercise is that you're considering questions an agent or publisher will ask if you want to submit a book proposal to a traditional, royalty-based publisher.

This exercise will take you from twenty to sixty minutes. It's a worthwhile investment that you will easily gain back throughout the writing and publishing process.

Your Assignment

1. Answer the questions below as completely and concisely as possible. The greater clarity you have around these questions, the better your book will be.
2. Go to www.david-sluka.com/resources and download a Word document with these nine questions or create your own document. Answer these questions as if you were submitting a book proposal to a publisher who wants to give you a generous advance to write your book and acquire it for publishing. In other words, do quality work.
3. Print out this sheet and put it up in a prominent place (next to the working title you created from the previous chapter).

* * * * *

1. Why are you writing the book? (What is your passion or motivation, and what is the book's purpose?)

2. What is the book about? (Summarize in one sentence. Then summarize in one or two paragraphs like you would see on the back cover of a book.)

3. What transformational effect will the book's content have on the reader? What are your book's benefits from your reader's point of view? What do readers learn? What solutions does it provide?

4. What are your qualifications to write on this topic? Why will a reader see you as credible to share your message?

5. Who is the specific audience for your book? Who will want to read it/buy it and why? (You may feel everyone should read your book, but be as specific as possible.)

6. How can you reach that audience? How will you promote and share the book?

7. What kind of platform do you have and what size is your audience right now? How many people are you reaching each year? (Followers of a blog, website, Facebook, Twitter, newsletter recipients, attendees at workshops, seminars, conferences, friends and connections with churches, businesses, etc.)

8. Are there similar books on the market? List them. What makes your book distinctive?

10. What interesting features could you include with your book that would help the reader get more out of your content? (For example, a study guide or questions for reflection; specific concepts you want the reader to take away from your chapter; action steps that help the reader apply your ideas; photographs, drawings, maps, charts, tables; appendices; other resources.)

CHAPTER 4

Get the Map

*Writing with clear purpose, focus, and organization
is a sure way to have readers follow you past your first chapter.*

When my kids were younger, they used to watch *Dora the Explorer* on TV. In each episode Dora embarks on an adventure with her talking backpack and monkey companion named Boots. Along their travels they always need direction and consult the Map. If there's anything I could shout out to you (like Dora always had her listeners do) that would help you write a better book, it would be, "Get a map!" and "Follow the map!"

Have you noticed that there is a negative stigma about creating and using an outline? I often use the word *map* or *structure* instead because the perception is that an outline makes writing stiff and stifles creativity and flow.

Let me say clearly that an outline does not cramp your style; it releases and empowers it.

An outline actually allows for greater creativity and flow because it provides the needed structure to hold what you want to say effectively with focus and organization.

The reason you can enjoy a hot drink is that there's a solid structure in place—your cup—to hold the liquid. With nothing to hold hot coffee, all you have is a mess—a hazardous, flowing mess. That's what happens if you just sit down to write without a structure in place to hold your inspiration. It may make sense to you, but it won't to those you want to reach with your message.

I never used to believe in outlines, even during the eight years I taught junior and senior high English. The main reason was that it's possible to write a decent paper (or a chapter in a book) without one. But after receiving thousands of dollars from writers to fix their book manuscripts written without one, I started helping authors map out their books on the front side of the project, saving them thousands of dollars in rewriting and editing costs. In each of these situations, I've always taken the author back to the first step of creating a clear map (like what I'm going to have you do) and then have them rewrite the book based on that map.

Not needing to use a map doesn't make you a better writer. An outline is not the training wheels on your bike that someday you get to remove.

I consider the outline more like the structure of your house, which is essential if you want your house to stand once you start building it. So please remember that following a map does not make you a weak or inexperienced writer. It makes you a wise one. And it guarantees you'll arrive where you want to go on time and in a good mood.

The better your map, the better your book.

Eight Benefits of a Book Map

Many who want to write a book have no idea what kind of work goes into preparation before a writer sits down to do what people would consider "writing a book."

I have to be honest. For many, creating a map is hard work and can even be painful. If you're the kind of person who just wants to sit down and let the inspiration flow, may I request that you consider an alternative approach. I promise the pain is short lived and you'll see the return on your investment almost immediately.

A few of the benefits of creating a map include:

- Before you officially start writing your content, you have a plan. You know with confidence where you're going and how you're going to get there.
- It helps you document what's inside your head. Have you ever said something for the first time, thinking it was clear in your mind, but once you said it, you found flaws and missing pieces? Often what's clear in your brain doesn't come out as clearly as you would hope. The mapping process gets your thoughts on paper so there are no bad surprises.
- When others find out you're writing a book and ask you, "So, what are you writing about?" you can give a clear and organized overview of your book, potentially turning listeners into future readers.
- A solid structure will allow your book to hold more information with a greater level of creativity in presentation.
- No writer's block. I have yet to have anyone experience writer's block when taking this approach.
- Your readers will thank you and will look forward to your next book. Because the content is focused and organized, it has greater power to accomplish your purpose for writing.
- Most if not all of your map will be used in the book in some way. So while you are making your map, you are actually writing your book.
- Added bonus: If you're going to submit your manuscript to a traditional publisher, they will ask for what I am going to help you to create.

I've just invested more than eight hundred words to try to convince you that a map is an essential tool if you want to write a great book. Please forgive your English teachers for making an outline the dreaded and seemingly useless part of the writing process. Hopefully you have a heightened awareness of its importance now and are more willing to put in the time and energy to set your book up for success.

If this book so far has been more tedious than empowering and you just want to get started, see Appendix A: I Just Want to Get Started.

For everyone else, the next two chapters will provide a few extra tips before you begin the writing process.

Your Assignment

1. Buy into the idea that a map for your book is more than a nice idea—it is an essential tool that will empower you to successfully communicate your content with others.

2. In the same document you wrote your working title(s), write a one-sentence summary of your book. For example, my one-sentence summary for this book is: *Write Your Book* is a step-by-step guide to prepare, write, and share a great nonfiction book.

3. Print out the page and put it up in a prominent place.

CHAPTER 5

Write Inspired and Write with God

Writing with inspiration brings to life information and experience
that others can enter into themselves. If God has given you
something to say, He wants to help you say it.

I believe there is strength outside of yourself that you can draw upon as you write. You don't have to just tough it out behind your computer to crank out your content. Below are five tips that can help you to write more inspired, which, by the way, is a much easier and more enjoyable way to write.

1. Ask God to help you.

I would like to suggest that God is just as interested in having you write your book as you are. I believe He is the one who has been forming this message in your heart in the first place, and if you're going to write about it, He wants to help.

Many people don't personalize God to this level, but I believe that He is interested in everything that pertains to our lives. God clearly likes multiplication (just look at nature), and there no better way to multiply the message He has given to you than to share it in a book that many can read without you present. God wants to write through you and with you.

Practically speaking, writing with God is a synthesis of His words and your words coming out as you write. Author and pastor Nathanael White says it this way:

God's Spirit carries us like wind in a sail, prompting us with new ideas that free us when we get stuck and sometimes add to the concepts we started with. God is light and we are like a colored lens over that light. So if the particular way we are made makes us like a red lens, when God's light shines through us, what people see is red light. They couldn't see the clear light that is God's pure presence, but once His light interacts with how He made us, it comes from us in a way that people recognize. The unique-to-us spectrum of color that comes from our relationship with God is what others will see when they read our writings, if we will simply ask Holy Spirit to help us in the process and follow Him as He leads. This result is something that we couldn't have done without God, but He wouldn't have done without us. This partnership is what takes our writing to a much higher level of power and potential for transformation."[1]

At the beginning of chapter 2, I told you about my amazing eighty-one-year-old friend and author who wrote her 130,000-word autobiography in 2012. Every morning Paula set aside ninety minutes to write. Before she began, she would say a short prayer, asking the Holy Spirit, "Dictate to me." Then she would write, combining her memory with a listening ear to inner promptings from God. As I edited her book I asked myself, *How could anyone remember this kind of detail and color about her past without using anything but a simple outline?* I then learned of her prayer.

God wants to help you write. Remember what He has spoken to you in the past, and be aware of how He is guiding your thoughts in that moment.

2. See the power of your testimony.

I look at nonfiction books as books of "testimony"—a public declaration of evidence and truth to something the author knows and/or has experienced that establishes a truth that others can enter into themselves if they choose.

In a court of law, testimonies are common and are critical to discovering the truth—usually the innocence or guilt of the defendant. The book of Revelation in the Bible speaks of a heavenly war against the "accuser" who accuses the righteous before God day and night. The Bible says that a person's testimony is one of the three elements used to combat this enemy (see Revelation 12:11).

The testimony you have today will have the same effect. When you tell your story—what you have learned and experienced, ways you have overcome—your testimony gives others faith to overcome. Your testimony is a powerful tool to empower others to have victory in the same area. This is why God wants to write with you, to share what He's given to you.

3. Capture creativity when it's happening.

Notice when words start flowing through your head and write them down. Don't think the creativity will come back when you have time. While I've tried to practice this, I still experience those moments when I say to myself in the middle of a burst of creativity, *Oh, I'll remember this later,* because the thoughts are so clear in that moment. I have yet to capture the same energy and content when I sit down even a few hours later to try to articulate what I was in the middle of just a few hours before.

---

1   Nathanael White, "Writing with God," June 11, 2013, personal e-mail. Used by permission. Connect with Nathanael at www.fathersheartbeat.org. Nathanael has also been an on-site editor and coach for my Write-Your-Book Workshop.

I wrote some of the content in this section before my shower this morning. I was in the bathroom, just about to shave, and realized I had stepped into a flow of creative thought. So I went to my computer and typed out a few thoughts so I could get back into the flow later. During my shower the first two sentences of this chapter kept going through my head, so I'm now sitting here in jeans and a T-shirt with my hair still a little wild.

At a minimum, take a minute and jot down a few notes, or have a digital recorder and record your idea so you can come back to it later. Notes taken when creativity is flowing will stir creativity when you're not feeling inspired. You can take the inspiration as your framework and then fill in the gaps with the details.

Take moments of inspiration as energy from God to push your book forward. This will help you to have inspired content when you're not feeling inspired. Right now I'm not feeling that inspired. But I have an outline that is telling me what I need to write next. Plus I'm drawing on information that I already know and what I wrote down yesterday when I was getting all the inspired thoughts while in the shower.

4. Set up your surroundings to avoid distraction, create focus, and support creativity.

If you're serious about stepping into a creative flow and getting a bunch of work done, turn off e-mail, your phone, text messaging, and social media, and find a place to work that gives you the privacy you need to focus.

Right now I am living outside the United States and we have a very small home. My desk is in the family room. Even though I have been working out of my home for over four years, it's still a trick to not be considered fair game for questions, problem solving, and interaction if I'm in the house. So my dedicated time to write is scheduled for when no one is home or when everyone is sleeping. When people are around, I choose to do parts of my book that I can work on with activity going on around me (e.g., formatting the text, copying and pasting content I'm using in this book from other resources I've written, and inserting footnote information).

5. Follow your map.

A good map allows you to write even when you don't feel inspired. It does not limit or quench creativity; it releases and empowers it. A map allows for greater inspiration and flow because it provides the needed structure to hold what you want to say effectively with focus and organization.

All creativity must fit somewhere in your map. If it doesn't, you need to alter your map to make room for it in its appropriate place. If your thoughts start to take you on a detour, write down the general idea so you can draw upon it later, but stay focused on the topic at hand. (I'll explain how to put these thoughts in the "parking lot" in the next chapter.) Following your map will ensure you arrive at your desired destination.

In the final chapter of this first section, let's look at a few more tips that will help make your writing efficient and fun.

Your Assignment

1. Take a moment right now to talk to God about your book. Tell Him about your vision for your book and ask for His help. Think about what "writing with God" looks like for you. Ask Him to write with you and through you.

2. Do you have a dedicated place to write that has limited distractions? Think about where you want to write your book. Start to make any needed adjustments in your setup at home or wherever you plan to write to avoid distraction, create focus, and support creativity.

3. Take the pieces of paper with your working title, your one-sentence summary, and your answers to the Nine Questions (from chapters 2, 3, and 4) and put them up at this dedicated place where you will be writing your book.

CHAPTER 6

Make Writing Efficient and Fun

*There's a better way to write. Either rent a charming villa in the
countryside, or make these twelve recommendations a part
of your writing to maximize your energy and creativity.*

Here are twelve tips to keep in mind as you begin the process of writing your book.

1. **Dedicate a specific time to write and prioritize it.** If this book is a priority for you, then other things will have to become a lower priority. For me everything seems like a number-one priority, so I try to do it all and multitask to the max. But this doesn't really work that well.

   Two things typically get in the way of a person writing a book: dedicated time to write and some assurance along the way that you're doing the right thing. I'm sharing with you a proven method to write your book. So now all you have to do is dedicate time to follow the steps in this book.

   Let's think through what kind of time you can dedicate to writing this book. Ask yourself the following questions and then fill out Appendix B: My Writing Timeline at the back of this book to give yourself a tentative timeline for your book.

   - **By what date do you want your book to be done?** You're more likely to finish your if you give yourself a goal to shoot for. Set your goal and then work backward to see how much you need to write per day to accomplish it.

   - **How long do you estimate your book to be?** Many people ask me how long their books should be. My answer is *As long as it needs to be to say what you want to say.* That may be twenty thousand words, seventy-five thousand words, or something in between. A longer, thicker book may seem more like a real book, but it's far better to say what you need to say and be done. I've read some books where the author could have used 50 percent fewer words with greater impact. So focus on making your content as good as it can be and let the length take care of itself.

   If you're concerned you may not have enough pages to make what you'd consider a real book, I encourage you to go to a bookstore and see the various sizes books can be. Most printers can create a book that is smaller than the typical 5.5 x 8.5 or 6 x 9 inches. Think outside the box. Being creative with book size and formatting of the text can give the book greater perceived value while still holding your content.

To calculate the approximate number of pages a paperback book will be, you can estimate that about 250 words fit on the printed page of a book that is 5.5 x 8.5 inches. So if your manuscript is forty thousand words, it'll be about 176 pages, depending on the interior layout of the text (in addition to a title page, copyright page, dedication, acknowledgments, and supplements the book may have, like a study guide, endnotes, and appendices).

A book that has forty thousand words usually contains ten to twelve chapters that are three thousand to four thousand words each. The chapters in this book range from just under one thousand (chapter 2) to three thousand (this chapter).

I've read excellent books that have fifty or more short chapters. The goal is not necessarily to write a certain number of words or have a certain number of chapters. Let what you have to say dictate the form the book takes and how many words there are.

- **How much time can you reasonably devote to following the instructions in this book to write your book?** Once a day for an hour during your most productive time? Once a week? Are you taking a sabbatical or a writing retreat and have most of your day devoted to your writing? I've found that most people can write about a page (250 words) in an hour. Many can write more than that, but this is a good starting place. If you set aside four to five days a week and write ninety minutes to two hours each day (this is the amount of time I've found works well for most authors), you can write 250 to 500 words per day and finish your manuscript in four to six months.

  Do the math, set some goals for yourself, and write those goals in Appendix B. Then hang up a piece of paper with these goals somewhere you can see them each day.

  After you have done your part with your manuscript (and if it is in good condition when it goes to the editor), allow about two months for editing, proofreading, interior pagination or typesetting, uploading files to a printer or print-on-demand service, printing, and shipping to your house. If you need more than a light edit and proofread, add an additional month. Appendix B has a timeline that I use with my clients once they are done with their manuscripts. This timeline represents my only doing a light edit and/or proofread.

2. **Write when you are at your best.** Past jobs I've had have forced me to be "on" at any given time during the day or night. But as I've paid attention to my natural disposition and preferences, I've

learned what time of day I'm most alert and energetic. When do you work best? You may get creativity boosts throughout the day, but you will notice your productivity increase when you set aside time to focus solely on the book-writing process during a time when you have the most energy and clarity of thought.

3. **Focus only on your book during your writing time.** Multitasking is a myth. Search that phrase on the Internet and you'll find a plethora of sources that support the fact that trying to do a number of things at the same time is not helpful for any of the tasks.[1] In fact you will perform each task more slowly and less accurately. So devote your full attention to your project and you'll make greater traction faster.

4. **Let the words flow.** Besides what I wrote in the last chapter about writing inspired and with God, here are a few tips to help you get into the creative flow. This is also super important for those who like their manuscripts to look just right as they are writing their books.

- **As you work, write whatever comes to mind to get on paper the content you have in your head right now.** This is not your final draft. I should probably say that again. Your first draft is not your final draft. All good writing is refined many times before the final product is what it should be. I like what Ray Edwards says: "Write recklessly, re-write ruthlessly."[2] Another way to say it is "First get it written, then get it right."[3]

- **Don't try to write, edit, and format at the same time.** When I say let the words flow, I mean to avoid self-editing or choose to edit very little. Creative flow uses a different side of your brain than editing or formatting the text. So if you have to do research before writing, focus on just that during your writing time. Then set aside time to simply freewrite, following your outline. Set aside another time for editing and another time for formatting. Avoid trying to do them all at the same time. This is the best advice I can give to you. So you may want to read this paragraph again.

  At this stage, you may make certain words **bold** or *italicized* to show emphasis. (Avoid using ALL CAPS for emphasis.) You will also insert paragraph breaks using the return or enter key. But that should be the extent of the formatting you do.

---

1 http://www.psychologytoday.com/blog/the-power-prime/201103/technology-myth-multitasking.

2 Ray Edwards is a marketing strategist, copywriter, speaker, and author. His very helpful website and blog is www.rayedwards.com.

3 James Scott Bell, Write Great Fiction: Plot & Structure, 2004-09-22 (Kindle Location 121). F+W Media, Inc.

I've received way too many Word documents that were formatted the way the author wanted them to look, but that created a ton of work for the person who had to do the pagination. Those authors did not use the tools in their word-processing software to insert page breaks or center titles on the page. Instead they hit the return key multiple times to get to the next page, used the space bar or tab key to center, or tapped the space bar to indent the first lines of paragraphs.

Earlier today I spent a few hours fixing endnotes (they are like footnotes but are placed at the end of the chapter or book instead of at the bottom of the page) that were entered manually instead of using the built-in feature in Word. I had to find each endnote number in the manuscript, remove it, insert the endnote properly, and copy and paste the endnote information from where it was to where it needed to be. I did this nearly fifty times.

I say all this because I want you to know that every touch on your computer's keyboard is a stroke you or someone else will have to process sometime in the future.

Professionals do not manually enter spaces between each of the paragraphs. They set up a style so the word-processing program puts in spaces automatically. (Notice how the paragraph before and after this one is formatted—with no first-line indent and a space between each paragraph.) This ensures consistency throughout the text.

Overly formatting your text—trying to get it to look exactly how you want it for the end product—will raise your costs. If you must do some formatting, keep it very simple. If you really like things looking good as you go along, I recommend three things:

— **Purchase a design template.** Visit www.bookdesigntemplates.com and purchase a book design template for Microsoft Word. These are great templates you can use not just to write your book but also to format it.

— **Format if don't feel like writing something new.** But allow yourself to get into a flow. When you talk to a good friend, you don't self-edit. You just unload. Do that in writing too.

— **Learn how to use the tools correctly in the word-processing program you're using**. Word, Pages, and other document programs have built-in tools. There are plenty of free resources on the Internet (including YouTube videos) that show how to use these tools. I still search out helpful resources every day and learn new and better ways to use the tools I have. One hour spent learning how to do something correctly and more efficiently will save you time for this book and for every other writing project you do in the future. So it's time well invested.

5. **Flow within your outline, not outside of it.** When I say to let it flow, it's not a free pass to write about anything and everything that comes to mind. It is permission to let the ideas flow within the constraints of your outline—the part of it you are writing at that time.

If you happen to step into the flow of another part of the book besides the one you had planned to work on, go with the flow. Today I was planning to finish up the previous chapter. But I stepped into a flow of thoughts about this chapter, so that's what I'm working on today. My outline is in place, so I know what I have to write about and I'll get to the other content later. But I'm using the natural energy I have right now to fuel this part of the book. It's coming together much more quickly than if I would have told myself, "You planned to finish chapter 4 today. You have to do chapter 4," and then suppressed the thoughts that were coming for this chapter.

I could have put some thoughts in the "parking lot" (see the next bullet), but the flow I am in right now is actually getting another part of this book done, which is the goal—to finish the book. So any flow that helps you to accomplish your ultimate goal of finishing your book is good. I probably would not be able to step back into the same flow when my schedule said it was time to work on chapter 5.

Just make sure that when you're flowing, you write that flow in the right spot in your outline. Or, if you prefer to learn the hard way, feel free to try to figure out where the content belongs later.

6. **Put unfocused thoughts in the parking lot.** You'll notice that when you step into creativity, you'll get a ton of creative thoughts about *everything*, not just the topic you're working on. Writing with focus takes discipline. There is nothing bad about having stray thoughts. Just don't let them distract you from what you're trying to focus on. But you also don't want to lose something good that you may want to use later.

Whether you are starting to think about something related or unrelated to the book, if it's not directly related to what you are working on at that moment, put it in the parking lot. When I conduct meetings or workshops, if someone brings up an issue or asks a question that is not directly related to what we're talking about, I write it down on a sheet of paper hanging on the wall so that I can address it later. That reassures the person that I'm going to deal with it, and it helps me remember the question or issue later. You can do the same thing. Have a piece of paper by your side or another file open on your computer to document anything you want to remember later but doesn't belong in what you are working on right now.

7. **Make yourself comfortable and enjoy yourself.** Work outside. Enjoy your favorite hot or cold beverage (but avoid spilling it on your computer). Put on music. (I avoid music with words and

stick mostly with classical music that is lively.[1]) Make a healthy snack to nibble on while you write. Buy a bunch of helium balloons or a bubble machine and have them floating around the room. Whatever makes your working environment more productive and enjoyable, do it. Get into your writing zone and kick out a bunch of <u>content</u>.[2]

8. **Write in 60-, 90-, or 120-minute blocks of time**. I find it hard to get into a decent flow in anything less than an hour. More than two hours, I start to lose the writing edge that is needed. If you set aside a half or full day to write, set an alarm for yourself so that you get up and take regular breaks. Those breaks will help you to be more productive when you dive back into the content afterward.

   British novelist, poet, and children's author Helen Dunmore has said, "A problem with a piece of writing often clarifies itself if you go for a long <u>walk</u>."[3] Take a break when you need to. That will often provide you with the fresh perspective you need. I find myself noodling on concepts throughout the day, and often something that I've been stumped on will all of a sudden become clear.

9. **Ask questions along the way.** There's nothing quite like doing a bunch of work and then realizing that you've wasted your time because you did it the wrong way. This book should provide most if not all of what you need to write your book. But always feel free to ask someone you'd consider to be a professional in the field or even someone who might know just a little more than you do.

10. **Capture creativity when it's happening.** I already wrote about this in the previous chapter, but it's worth repeating. Pay attention when ideas start to come to mind. Take time at that moment to write them down—at least the general idea or a few bullet points. Otherwise your ingenious thoughts that were once so clear will disappear into the dark and mysterious abyss that holds all the creativity that didn't get captured in the moment.

11. **Don't get stuck in the weeds.** This goes along with my earlier point about letting the words flow. During your writing, avoid spending a bunch of time trying to say it just right, documenting references for footnotes, writing out quotations or Scriptures, doing research, etc. For content that requires documentation of some kind, insert a footnote or endnote right away so you can find the spot later and follow copyright law by documenting your sources correctly. Be sure to use the Insert Footnote tool in your word-processing program. But in the footnote itself just type "Insert footnote here."

---

1   Currently on my playlist is "Mozart for Brain Power" by London Festival Orchestra.

2   This is a great blog post by Beth Barany about taking care of yourself while you are writing: <u>www.writers-funzone.com/blog/2013/06/26/writers-give-to-yourself-first-by-beth-barany.</u>

3   <u>www.guardian.co.uk/books/2010/feb/20/ten-rules-for-writing-fiction-part-one</u>; <u>www.brainpickings.org/index.php/2012/11/09/helen-dunmore-rules-of-writing/</u>.

For the footnote in the previous chapter for Nathanael White, I typed in the footnote area "Insert contact information for Nathanael White." It was tempting for me to send an e-mail to him at the moment or try to search for his website. Instead I stayed in the flow and put that task in the parking lot.

If you're quoting someone or using Scripture to support your point, you can make notes in your text like "Put the Dr. James quote here" or "Quote John 3:16–17 here." If you're writing and realize that your content needs some supporting documentation that you need to research, just type "Support this point" or "Research this more" and move on to what is already in your head. So that you can find these gaps to fill in later, I recommend using the highlighting function in your word-processing program so you can find it easily. This will keep you in the flow while still marking where you need to go back and do something later.

12. **Do whatever you have to do to make significant progress.** Each person has his or her own way of working most productively. Figure that out for yourself and make it work. If your way goes against any of what I've shared, I would ask you to reconsider your productivity habits. All that I've shared is well supported by productivity experts.

However, if you write better at a standing desk wearing a plaid bow tie with jazz guitar music playing in the background next to a big carnival teddy bear, go for it. Or maybe it's better for you to dictate your book into a digital recorder and then have someone transcribe the text. Go for it. Regardless of what you do, figure out fast what works for you and do it. Others are waiting to read your book! So let's get started.

Your Assignment

1. Fill out Appendix B: My Writing Timeline at the back of this book to give yourself a tentative timeline for your book. Then post a copy of your plan where you have the printed documents from previous assignments.
2. Purchase any tools that are going to help your writing process (e.g., background music without words, a design template, your favorite healthy drink or snack).

Step 1: Prepare

A Map Will Get You There

The next three sections of this book will take you from your book concept to a book in your hands to share with others. These three sections are:

- Prepare
- Write
- Share

This is how I group the services I provide to authors, and they are also the three parts of my Write-Your-Book workshops.[1]

In *Step 1: Prepare*, I'm going to help you create your plan, your map, your outline. Call it whatever you want, but we're going to make a great one for your book. The next five chapters are a worthy investment. If structure grates against your personality, remember that a good structure actually strengthens the opportunity for greater innovation and flexibility because focus and organization are in place. So hang in there and do the work. You'll be *really* happy you did (and so will your readers).

If you take one day for each of these Prepare steps (or two if necessary on some), you will be ready to write your book in one week. Go for it!

Step 2: Write will show you how to do what people usually think of when they imagine writing a book. With a good map in place, this step will go as quickly as the time you are able to set aside to write and edit.

Step 3: Share is about how you share your book with others. I'll show you how you can publish and print your book on your own, publish with the help of a self-publishing company, or pursue a traditional publisher.

The only way for your book to get written is if you start writing. So open a word-processing document and let's get writing!

---

1   See www.write-your-book.com for more details.

CHAPTER 7

Prepare Step 1:

Create a Working Title and Subtitle

"A great title will not sell a bad book, but a poor title
will hide a good book from potential customers." —Dan Poynter

According to eye-tracking research, it takes less than two-tenths of a second for a person to form a first impression of a website. A viewer takes about 2.6 seconds to land on the area of a website that most influences his or her first impression.[1] When it comes to books, the title and subtitle (along with the front cover design) is what will influence the first impression to a potential reader. Since you have less than three seconds, these elements must be good.

In chapters 16 and 17 I'll talk about designing a great book cover. For now, let's focus on your title and subtitle. I love what Dan Poynter says about book titles:

A great title will not sell a bad book, but a poor title will hide a good book from potential customers.[2]

If you look at the best-selling nonfiction titles on the New York Times list right now,[3] you'll see quite a mixture of approaches on book titling. Some authors use a rather obscure title with a subtitle that helps explain what the book is about. Seth Godin's book *Purple Cow* doesn't tell you much until you read the subtitle, *Transform Your Business by Being Remarkable*. Malcom Gladwell's *Blink* doesn't make much sense until you read *The Power of Thinking Without Thinking*. Other titles say exactly what the book is about, albeit in a creative way, so that it's very clear to potential readers what they're buying.

---

1   Andrew Careaga, "Eye-tracking Studies: First Impressions Form Quickly on the Web," Missouri S&T News and Events, February 14, 2012, http://news.mst.edu/2012/02/eye-tracking_studies_show_firs/.

2   Dan is an amazing resource for writing, producing, and promoting your book, and also starting your own publishing business. See www.parapublishing.com.

3   www.nytimes.com/best-sellers-books/.

If you look at various lists of the best-selling nonfiction books of all time,[1] you'll notice that the titles and subtitles work together to give a pretty clear picture of what the book is about. There's not much guessing that needs to be done with *How to Win Friends and Influence People*, *Think and Grow Rich*, *The Common Sense Book of Baby and Child Care*, *The 7 Habits of Highly Effective People*, *The Power of Positive Thinking*, or *What to Expect When You're Expecting*. Other titles, like *Who Moved My Cheese?*, *What Color is Your Parachute?*, *Rich Dad, Poor Dad*, *Please Don't Eat the Daises*, or *Roots*, leave more (sometimes a lot more) to the imagination.

With millions of titles on the market, it can be tough to find a unique title that describes your book well yet is distinct, creative, and has a hook (it's catchy).

It's risky to go with an obscure title. Known authors, or writers with a strong marketing plan, can get away with it more easily than someone who's self-publishing for the first time. It's also harder for Internet search engines to detect your book if the key topic isn't in the title itself. If you want to take the risk and attempt to set a new trend, go for it. Just adjust for the risks.

While it's challenging to be completely original, and sometimes it's detrimental to be too out of the box, it's always possible to put a fresh spin on something common. I've talked to a number of pastors who want to write a book about hearing God's voice. The title inevitably is *How to Hear God's Voice* or something similar. Unfortunately, that title doesn't communicate anything fresh.

Sometimes when I'm working with authors on their titles, it seems like we're trying to come up with the next new shiny object. I end up asking myself, *Why can't people just realize what's good for them and take the medicine instead of having to woo people with fancy titles and attractive designs?* I, and you too, want to act with integrity and avoid marketing manipulation. But the other side of the coin is what Dan Poynter's quote at the start of this chapter states so well. A poor title will hide a good book from people who really want it and who need the content that's inside. So it's well worth your effort to make your title as good as it can be so that at least you're not putting a hindrance in anyone's way from buying your book.

Nat Bodian, book marketing expert and author of *How to Choose a Winning Title*, says, "Choose a title for your book at least as carefully as you would select a given name for your firstborn child."[2] It's worth taking some time to name your book. If you want to read more about creating a

---

1   See http://blog.nathanbransford.com/2013/09/bestselling-nonfiction-books-by-year.html. On this page there is a link to where it is on Time's website: www.goodreads.com/list/show/12719.Time_Magazine_s_All_TIME_100_Best_Non_Fiction_Books. A list of New York Times best sellers is here: www.hawes.com/no1_nf_d.htm

2   Dan Poynter, "How to Name Your Nonfiction Book," excerpted with permission from Writing Nonfiction: Turning Thoughts into Books by Dan Poynter (Santa Barbara, CA: Para Publishing, 2000), www.xlibris.com.au/authors-lounge-how-to-name-nonfiction-book.aspx.

good title for your book, I recommend an article called "How to Name Your Nonfiction Book" by Dan Poynter.[3]

Ten Tips to Choose a Good Title and Subtitle

A successful title and subtitle will create understanding to let the reader know what your book is about and generate interest. My ten tips for choosing a good title and subtitle are as follows:

1. **Have fun and be creative.** If you're writing an autobiography, *My Life* isn't going to work well for you unless you're former president Bill Clinton or some other famous celebrity. Choose a title that will mean something to more than those closest to you. Think outside the box a bit and have fun with it.

2. **Consider your book title to be a "hook,"** similar to what a catchy lyric and tune is to the chorus of a song. Ask yourself, *What is the main message (the slogan, the chorus, the one word or short catch phrase) that I want going through people's heads after they read my book?*

3. If your book's topic is a main theme you speak about, or a series you want to develop (like *The Power of a Praying…* series by Stormie Omartian or the *Rich Dad, Poor Dad* series by Robert Kiyosaki), consider that you're doing more than coming up with a book title. **You're creating your brand.**

4. If you're writing on a well-known topic, **choose a title that articulates your fresh or revelatory spin** on the topic.

5. As a general rule, **keep the title short.** You don't need to tell the whole story. You just need to create curiosity and some sort of understanding so readers know what they're getting.

6. **Stay positive.** In general, people are looking for a solution to a problem, not a prolonged discussion about the problem itself. If you or your child has nightmares, which book are you more likely to pick up—*Terrors of the Night* or *Sweet Dreams Every Night*? There's nothing wrong with stating the problem; just don't leave people there. Two former colleagues at Best Buy called their book *Why Work Sucks and How to Fix It*.[4] That title acknowledges the frustration that many in the workplace have, but also lets readers know the book provides a solution to the problem.

7. **Paint a picture of the end result.** This goes along with the previous point about staying positive. One of the authors I work with wrote and self-published a book

---

3   Ibid.

4   By Cali Ressler and Jodi Thompson. See www.gorowe.com/.

called <u>Rejection Exposed</u>.[1] We are presently pitching the book to a traditional publisher, but the acquisitions editor said she preferred the title of *Rejection Healed*. This is an awesome example about not only staying positive, but also zeroing in on the end result—where readers will end up if they read your book and do what it says.

8. **Use a subtitle to complement or describe your title**, especially if your title does not tell the reader exactly what the book is about. Create a picture for potential readers to know what to expect or what benefits they will receive by reading your book.

9. **View your title and subtitle from your audience's point of view.** You can love it, but if others do not, you're the only one who will enjoy your book. This is why it's so important to know who your audience is or who specifically you want your audience to be.

10. Remember **it's a working title**, not necessarily your final one. It's okay to have more than one working title. Be sure to print it out and put it up where you can see it often and ponder what the best title and subtitle for your book will be.

Your Assignment

1. Open the document that contains your working title and subtitle.

2. Quickly review the ten tips to choosing a good title and subtitle, and circle a few tips that most apply to you. Ask yourself, *What do I want my title to say in a word or a short phrase, and how can I communicate that in a way that appeals to my audience?*

3. Look at your working title and subtitle and make adjustments as needed. Type out variations of your title and subtitle if needed.

4. On a new page, type your working book title and subtitle at the top of the page or in the header of your document, which will cause it to show up on every page. (See the graphic below for an example.)

5. Print out the page and put it up where you will see it often.

---

1   See Anthony Hulsebus's website, <u>dominionministries.net</u>, for this book and other resources to deal with rejection in your life. You can read an excerpt from his book at <u>www.david-sluka.com/2013/10/29/so-whats-your-problem-discerning-the-root-of-the-fruit-you-hate-by-anthony-hulsebus/</u>.

6. Send an e-mail to a trusted friend or a few friends who know you and share with them the topic of your book. It would be helpful if those people represented the audience you are trying to reach. Ask for their feedback and recommendations.

7. You might nail the title and subtitle right away. If so, great! But over the time that you're writing your book, additional ideas may come. Capture the creativity of the moment and write them down *right away*. By the time you're done writing your manuscript, the title should be pretty clear and you can choose which one you want to go with.

8. If you haven't yet purchased the book *Platform* by Michael Hyatt, do so today. You want to be building your platform while you write your book.

Write Your Book

Your Step-By-Step Guide to Write and Publish a Great Nonfiction Book

CHAPTER 8

Prepare Step 2:

Create Chapter Titles

*The title of your chapter will set the tone for the content that follows,
so make a grand entrance.*

When people are thinking about buying your book, they will get a feel for your book by looking at three things:

- Front cover (the title, subtitle, and cover design)
- Back cover (description of your book, recommendations, author bio)
- Table of contents (your chapter titles and any additional description of what's in the book)

Because of this, it's worth it to invest time creating chapter titles that promote your book well and make browsers want to buy your book to read more.

After you complete your assignment at the end of this chapter, you will have the most basic of outlines in place and a working table of contents for your book. With one glance at one piece of paper, you should be able to see clearly the scope of your book.

To determine your chapter titles, complete either of the statements below. (There are a number of ways to ask the same question. Use whichever helps you to break down your content into chapter divisions.)

- The ten (or whatever number) things I want to talk about in my book are …
- Or: The main topics that I want to talk about are …

A Few Approaches to Naming Your Chapters

The chapter title sets the tone for the content that follows, so make a grand entrance. Below are a few approaches for writing nonfiction chapter titles. Choose the one(s) that works best for the book you are writing, or go with another approach if it fits your book better.

- **Creative statement or description.** Be creative and have fun, but avoid cute titles that do not clearly describe what the chapter is about. Let your chapter titles demonstrate the unique insight or approach you have on your topic.

- **Start with an action.** Because my book is a how-to book, most of my chapter names start with an action of some kind. A self-help book might also have chapter names that start with an action, showing the reader the basic steps outlined in the book.
- **Statements in logical sequence.** Whatever kind of nonfiction book you are writing, there is usually a logical sequence to divide out your content that will make sense to the reader.
- **Chronological.** Autobiographies are often laid out chronologically, so the chapter titles could be creative names for different periods or key events in your life.
- **Principles.** A book that teaches principles may be divided out by the main lessons to be learned, in the order a reader will need to read them. So the chapter titles would be creative ways to describe each of those principles.
- **Steps.** A how-to book can be divided into steps to complete a task, so each chapter title would be a clear and concise description of each step.

Your First Draft Is Not Your Final Draft

I'm not sure where I heard it, but many, many times growing up I heard, *Your first draft is not your final draft.* As an English teacher, I had far too many students who tried to write the final draft of their papers in the first pass. I personally tend to self-edit as I go along instead of just letting the words flow onto paper as if I were talking to someone. This approach will not give you your best work.

Take the approach of just getting down on paper initial thoughts as quickly as possible. This will give you the raw content that will serve as a good foundation for your book. The refinement process of editing is what will make your book truly shine. If you try to edit as you go or think through everything before you write, your writing will feel stiff and calculated.

Consider this as you write your chapter titles today: they do not have to be final. They only represent the main topics and how the book is divided.

Type out the basic topics you want to cover and adjust them until you are satisfied that they cover most if not all of the content in your book. Then go back over them, but this time think of how you can say the same thing more creatively.

The level of excellence you demonstrate in your table of contents is a signal to potential readers what they can expect with the rest of the book. So don't put your readers to sleep while they're at your table of contents.

Ensure that each chapter title clearly supports the title and subtitle of your book. As you step into creativity while thinking about your chapter titles, you might even "accidentally" find your book title.

Another Approach

Mindmapping is another approach to brainstorming and organizing the content of your book. This method makes more sense to some people. If you're having a hard time with my approach, I encourage you to read the article "How to Use a Mindmap to Start Your Book" by Nina Amir.[1]

To learn more about mindmapping see www.mindmapping.com. You can also download software from the Internet to help you map your ideas. Check out these free downloads:

- www.thebrain.com
- www.xmind.net

Your Assignment

1. In the same document where you have your title and subtitle, type out the basic topics you want to cover and adjust them until you are satisfied that they cover most if not all of the content in your book. Or use the mindmapping method to brainstorm the main topics you want to cover in your book. Consider what naming approach(es) from my list above will work best for your book.

2. At this point, don't worry about how many chapters you have. Just ensure that the main points you want to cover are represented in your chapter titles. Note that I divided my chapters into sections to further organize my book and help the reader know even more clearly the different parts of my book. This approach worked best for this book. Determine how best to organize your book and the natural divisions that will serve as a solid structure to hold your writing.

3. Put your chapter titles in the format of the sample on the next page (taken from the table of contents of this book). Try to get everything on *one* piece of paper like a table of contents. Lessen the font size if needed, but get it on one page so you can see the scope of your book at a glance.

4. Review your chapter titles, but this time think of how you can say the same thing more creatively. Change any that need to be stated differently. Let your chapter titles demonstrate the unique insight or approach you have on your topic.

5. Print out the page and put it up where you will see it often. You now have a basic plan for your book in place.

6. Let this outline sit for a day or two. Then come back to it and review it.

7. Make adjustments to your map as needed. Don't move on until you are at least 90 percent sure your map outlines your book the way you want it to be.

---

1   www.thefutureofink.com/mindmap-to-start-your-book.

Write Your Book

Your Step-By-Step Guide to Write and Publish a Great Nonfiction Book

CHAPTER 9

Prepare Step 3:

Develop an Elevator Pitch for Each Chapter

Each chapter's description is a tight pitch that lands the purpose for the chapter with a clear, concise, and captivating description inviting readers to invest their time in the chapter's content.

If you had fifteen to thirty seconds to tell me what your book was about, could you give me an articulate pitch that would pique my interest and make me want to know more? Most people can ramble on for a while about the topic they want to write about, but rarely do I find anyone ready to pitch me his or her book with a clear and convincing summary, even after writing the full manuscript.

What would you do if you had a two-minute interview on the national morning talk show of your choice? The host asks you, "So, I just loved chapter three. Please tell our viewers what it's about." Could you nail a summary in two short sentences? (Have you ever noticed that the person being interviewed never talks for more than twenty to thirty seconds at a time and only responds with talking points, not a narrative?)

This chapter is all about developing an "elevator pitch" for each chapter. An elevator pitch is a summary that you'd be able to give someone if he or she got on an elevator with you at the bottom floor, and you had to clearly land your point before the elevator door opens where you want to get off.

Please note that I use the terms *elevator pitch, summary, synopsis, sound bite, sales copy,* and probably a few others interchangeably. While each has its own nuance of meaning, through this exercise I'm trying to help you write a *summary* of your chapter that is a good *synopsis* you could share quickly, like in an *elevator,* that is convincing and attractive enough to be a *sales pitch.*

Six Benefits of Chapter Summaries

The work you'll do in this step will accomplish the following:

1. It forces you to clearly say what your chapter is about. Often a reader is confused about what the author is trying to say because the author is unsure of what he or she wants to say. This exercise takes care of that. You'll have a clear statement that summarizes the essence of each chapter.

2. This summary will focus your chapter and help align the content that goes into it.

3. The summary can also serve as a sound bite or talking point for sales copy, interviews, and key quotations you may want to pull from the book.

4. It will explain *why* that chapter is important and *what* action the reader may need to take as a result.

5. A short summary of each chapter can be included in the table of contents, giving a potential reader a greater understanding of what your book is about.

6. If you are planning to pitch your book to an agent or publisher via a proposal, these chapter descriptions will be required and will clearly tell a publisher if you have your act together as a writer. The ability to write clearly using fewer words usually demonstrates that you can write well using more words.

More Than a Synopsis—Make Your Sales Pitch

Each chapter's elevator pitch is more than just a synopsis. Consider it your key talking point or the sales copy you would use to sell the chapter. Even if you're not interested in how many copies your book sells or doing interviews with your book, taking time to craft these chapter summaries will focus and organize your book—for your sake and for the sake of your readers. In just a few sentences you can create a clear target to hit as you're writing the chapter.

Have you ever heard a great speaker, but at the end of the speech you weren't sure what the person said, you just knew they said it well? It's great that you were entertained, but what are you taking away from the talk? Most nonfiction books have a purpose, and the purpose is more than just entertainment. Usually the author is hoping the reader will respond in some way to the information presented in the book. Specific action requires clear direction.

A clear summary of your chapter articulated like a sales pitch will paint the target you're going to hit with your chapter's content.

Six Tips for a Good Elevator Pitch

This exercise is not easy. It can be fun if you get into the groove and if you have a propensity for advertising. But anyone can do it, so have fun narrowing and refining your message into a few powerful sentences.

Here are six tips to writing a good description for your chapter:

1. **Consider the benefit of the chapter for your reader, not just the feature.** For example, a book about child care will have some great *information* about how to choose the right child care for your toddler. This information is the *feature*, not the end benefit to the reader; it's just the means to a greater end. The end *benefit* is the peace of mind your readers can get when they find someone who will properly care for their children. State that benefit in your summary. There is a big difference between "There are five steps to choosing a good day-care provider" and "Finding

good child care will bring you peace of mind, knowing your child is not only receiving great care but is also developing healthily as a child."

Since this is such an important point, let me give you one more example. When I worked in the retail training department at Best Buy Co., we taught the sales team to help customers see the benefits, not just give them technical features. I had the opportunity to see this training in action during a recent personal purchase. I needed to buy a nice camera to take with me on a trip with my family. Instead of using terms like megapixel resolution, ISO range, AF tracking, LCD monitor, optical viewfinder, and HD, the salesperson focused on explaining the *benefits* of the features instead—that I'd be able to enlarge a special picture without losing quality to put up in the living room, for example. This approach was a lot more successful—for both of us.

Why do people want to read your book? Because it will benefit *them* in some way. If they don't see a benefit, they will not pick up your book. Look at the content of your book from your reader's perspective. Make it easy for people to pick up your book by stating the benefits for them. Features are great, but be sure to connect any feature you state to its respective benefits.

If you look at my table of contents or the italicized sentences at the start of each of my chapters, you'll see that I attempted to state the benefit of my chapters to the reader, not just the content each chapter contains.

State the benefits of your chapter's content clearly for the reader.

2. **Write the description like sales copy or a sound bite.** Don't start with "This chapter is about …" or "In this chapter I'm going to talk about …" Sell the reader on the content of each chapter. Even if you're not interested in how much money you make on your book, writing these descriptions with this in mind will raise the excellence of your writing and force you to be convinced your chapter is worth writing before you start to write. The goal is to create an articulate summary that captures readers' attentions and makes them want to read more.

3. **Keep the description from two to five sentences.** You don't need to give the reader all the information. It's just a preview of *what* they will read and *how* it will benefit them to read it. Land your main point and move on.

4. **Get help if needed.** If you're having a hard time doing this, have someone ask you (or imagine someone asking you), "What is this chapter about?" Write down your response.

5. **Write what comes to mind quickly for an initial summary of each chapter.** Then take time to review what you've written and sharpen it up. During my workshops I

give participants about thirty minutes to complete this exercise. Most get it done in that time.

6. **Make one main point in each chapter.** That one main point should be clearly understood in your summary. Let's look at that next.

Make One Main Point

In Andy Stanley's wonderful book *Communicating for a Change: Seven Keys to Irresistible Communication*, he says, "Every time I stand to communicate I want to take one simple truth and lodge it in the heart of the listener. I want them to know that one thing and know what to do with it."[1] I believe this strategy should also be followed when writing a chapter. Communicate one main point so well that it stays with readers long after they close the book. Your chapter description should reflect this focus.

Consider your chapter to be a connect-the-dots coloring sheet (the kind children use that have numbered dots on a page and the child draws a line to connect 1 to 2 to 3 to 4 and so on until the dots form a clear picture). You may communicate a number of points (or dots) in your chapter, but at the end of your chapter, all of those points should be clearly connected so that your readers sees *one* simple truth. That one simple truth is what your chapter summary should describe.

My natural bent is that of a teacher. I look at information and quickly see how to break it down into main points, why they're important, what to do with them, and how to make what may be complicated more simple to understand. The downside of being a teacher (or a leader who has a lot to say) is seeing all the points of information that could be communicated, but knowing that no one will remember anything (or act on it) if I don't distill all I want to say down to one main point. I can make a number of points—like the dots on the coloring page—but they all have to support and submit to one main point that is meaningful to the listener.

Andy Stanley recognizes Howard Hendricks, who taught leaders to ask the question "So what?" After you write your chapter description, read it out loud and ask yourself, "So what? Why does this chapter matter to the audience I'm writing to?" If you don't have a good answer to that question, either you're addressing the wrong audience for your book or you need to rewrite the description better, focusing on the needs of those you're trying to reach with your book.

Using the child-care example above, *so what* if you have five steps to choose a good day-care provider? Some will say there are three and others will say there are ten. What I really care about is getting peace of mind, knowing my child is receiving great care and developing healthily as a child.

It's also important that you help your readers know what to do with what you've said—how they can take action for a desired change. Andy credits Rick Warren for asking a follow-up question

---

1   Andy Stanley and Lane Jones, *Communicating for a Change: Seven Keys to Irresistible Communication* (New York, NY: The Doubleday Religious Publishing Group, 2008), 12.

to "So what?": "Now what?"[2] Theory is nice and many people draw comfort from information. But a world of information does not solve any problems until people make good choices with corresponding actions in response to good information.

So if there is a "Now what?" in your chapter—an action that will make life better for the reader—include that in your elevator pitch. Having five steps to choose good child care is the "Now what?" Peace of mind and a healthy child is the "So what?"

Connect the Dots for Your Readers

Realize that in *your* mind, all your points are connected and interconnected because you are familiar with your topic and the ideas that support it. However, most readers are not going to connect the dots as readily. One of my pet peeves is when authors or speakers assume their audiences know information and therefore refer to it without explanation (e.g., a preacher who mentions a Bible character's name, assuming everyone in the audience knows the back story; or a leader who mentions a prominent political figure and a current event, presuming that everyone has heard about it on the news).

All writers say they want to reach new audiences with their messages, but rarely do they acknowledge that someone new might be in the crowd and take an extra minute to provide context so the information makes sense to a newcomer. Unless you're writing to a very specific audience and it is clear that knowledge of certain information is a precursor for your book (like a course where there are 101, 201, 301 levels), assume your readers don't know.

Be sure to connect the dots for your readers by connecting your points into one clear point. That clear point is going to be stated in your elevator pitch for your chapter.

Samples

Below are chapter descriptions that have come from some participants of my workshops or from people I've helped to write a book. (A warm thank you to each of them for giving me permission to share his or her content with you.)

Note that most of the descriptions have the following two components:

1. *What* the chapter is about, or *what* is the central truth or point of the chapter—a brief and engaging description of the chapter's content.
2. *Why* the chapter is important—*how* the content benefits the reader from the reader's point of view (per tip 1 in Six Steps for a Good Elevator Pitch above).

---

2   Andy's footnote says, "Howard Hendricks taught us to ask, 'So what?' Rick Warren is the first person I heard use the question, 'Now what?'" Andy Stanley, *Communicating for a Change: Seven Keys to Irresistible Communication* (New York, NY: The Doubleday Religious Publishing Group, 2008).

It'll take a little time to read through the following examples. I've included more than just a few so you can get a feel for what your chapter description might sound like. They all include the *what* and the *why* in some way. After reading each description, notice that it's pretty easy to know the one main thing the author is going to talk about in his or her chapter.

Below you will see the title the author gave the chapter and then his or her short description. After the descriptions you will find Your Assignment.

Chapter #__: Talent Never Takes a Vacation[1]

You can't win big without talent. Any great coach has great players, and any great leader has great people around them.

Chapter #__: 7 Steps to Forgive Yourself[2]

Forgiving yourself is no easy task. It requires an intentional and ongoing decision to choose life, embrace humility, and put justice in God's hands. Learning to be your own best friend leads to an ethical, authentic life.

Chapter #__: Don't You Love Me?[3]

How can a love that seemed so good go so bad? Broken love stories abound in our world, and no one starts out wanting to be the next casualty of love.

Note: This chapter opens Mark's book and introduces readers to his topic. He does this through telling stories and asking questions. But he still makes only one clear point: amid great intentions, love can end in tragedy and you don't want that to happen to you.

---

1   From a manuscript in process, *The Sixth Man* (working title), © 2013 Jerry Busone and David Sluka. Used by permission. Scheduled to be released spring 2014. Connect with Jerry at www.linkedin.com/in/jerrybusone or www.offthebenchleadership.com.

2   From *Like Yourself, Love Your Life: Overcome Big Mistakes & Celebrate Your True Beauty*, © 2011 Audrey Meisner. Used by permission. Audrey and her husband, Bob, are hosts of the television program It's A New Day, which can be streamed 24/7 on the Internet at www.mynewday.tv. Connect with Audrey at www.bobandaudrey.com.

3   From a manuscript in process, *Learning Love* (working title), © 2013 Mark Spencer. Used by permission. Mark has a master's degree in marriage and family therapy. Connect with Mark at www.markrspencer.com.

Chapter #__: Build Right from the Ground Up[4]

The path to becoming an Unlikely Hero starts with a commitment to the process of being conformed to the image of Christ, who was the servant of all. Your character is made in a Crock-pot, not a microwave, and godly character is the foundation for genuine and long-term success.

Chapter #__: A Look at My Roots[5]

My brother, Bill, once asked my dad, "Were there any heroes in our family?" His response was no. However, Dad's grandfather on his mother's side was Lieut. Col. Trowbridge. He was the first Union officer to use an African-American soldier as a Regiment in the Civil War in its fight against the Confederate Army.

Chapter #__: What Is Love Anyway?[6]

We all have a throbbing craving for love, but how we define, picture, give, and receive it is uniquely us. Just what does "real love" look like?

Chapter #__: Sweet Fragrance[7]

Our prayers are sweet-smelling incense unto the Lord. He wants us to pray, and He loves it when we pray.

Chapter #__: O.M.G.[8]

Do yourself and your team a big favor: know what others need through <u>O</u>bservation, <u>M</u>onitoring their progress, and <u>G</u>iving timely feedback—all the time. O.M.G. limits undesirable surprises and creates a culture for success.

---

4 From *Unlikely Hero: The Road to Extraordinary,* © 2011 Duncan Robinson (Maricopa: InGod Press, 2011), 51. Used by permission. Buy Duncan's book or e-book at your favorite online retailer or <u>here</u> at Amazon.com. Connect with him at <u>www.duncanrobinson.net</u>.

5 From a manuscript in process, © 2013 David McQuoid. Used by permission.

6 Mark Spencer, op. cit.

7 From a book Lou Bardal is presently writing on the power of speaking in tongues. © 2013 Lou Bardal. Used by permission. Lou has worked as a middle-school English teacher and a chemical-dependency counselor. She has been retired from counseling since 2011.

8 Jerry Busone, op. cit.

Chapter #___: Kingdom of God Ambassadors[1]

Jesus founded His kingdom on earth, beginning the restoration of God's Blueprint. We are called to be ambassadors for the KOG. We have been given authority and responsibility over everything on earth to establish justice. The KOG is not an enclosed church building, but rather a place of equipping from which we are sent out as ambassadors of His name, His power, and His purpose.

Chapter #___: The Setup for Shame[2]

I craved an escape. In desperation, I created a mess through trying too hard to get approval, busyness, and stuffing my feelings. In the middle of my mess I found hope and faced the irreversible consequences head on.

Chapter #___: Process of Transformation[3]

Transformation is a process through which we learn to love God, yield to His ways, and serve His purpose. This process conquers self-exaltation, self-reliance, and self-ambition, or in other words, the kingdom of the world. It is the process through which we learn to trust God as we experience His love, blessing, and truth in our lives. Transformation happens as a result of experiencing relationship with God.

Introduction[4]

Hollywood makes a living turning nobodies into somebodies who change the course of history. For a moment we are captured by the hope we can be that person. It is time to fantasize less about our favorite superhero and focus more on our Ultimate Hero. It is time for Christians to be refreshed by our great and powerful God and get on His road to the extraordinary.

---

1   From *The Blueprint: God's Design for Your Life* by Diane Kukala (San Diego: TJ Associates, LLC, 2013), 173. Used by permission. Diane is founder and chief leadership officer of Blueprint Leadership. Buy Diane's book and connect with her at www.theblueprintgodsdesign.com or www.blueprintleadership.com.

2   Audrey Meisner, op. cit.

3   Diane Kukala, op. cit., 217.

4   Duncan Robinson, op. cit., 11.

Chapter #__: The Legend of the Red Rock and Nearby Sunday School[5]

Rev. Kavanaugh established a Methodist mission to be used for Sunday school on the shores of the Mississippi, in Newport, an "arrow shot" away from the holy stone called Red Rock. This Sunday school house became the "place of meeting" for over one hundred years of camp meetings.

Chapter #__: Realistic Goal-Setting[6]

What is your dream and what can you actually manage? World domination is not accomplished in one camping trip! Embrace relevance, meaning, and cost counting. Listen to the Spirit of God, and befriend wise counsel to produce manageable and extraordinary goals.

Chapter #__: Playing a Game You Can't Win[7]

To the degree we buy into the lie that our performance alters God's opinion of us, we engage in a game we can't win. The only way to win this game is to choose not to play.

Chapter #__: What about Good Works?[8]

Even though we can't obtain favor and approval from God by what we do, we were created to do good works. They will naturally flow forth from a heart that embraces the exceptionally good news of grace.

Your Assignment

1. Follow the six tips in this chapter to write an elevator pitch for each chapter (set aside about an hour to do this). Be sure to ask the question "So what?" after each to ensure your chapter is connecting with the needs of your audience and making one clear point.

2. Start with the introduction. You may not be planning to include an introduction in your book, but write the elevator pitch for your introduction as if it will be

---

5 From a manuscript in process, *Minnesota: The Revival State: When the Frozen Chosen Were Not So Frozen* (working title), © 2012 Dale Gilmore. Used by permission. You can contact Dale at dalegil@msn.com.

6 From a manuscript in process, *Spiritual Scouting: Journey into God through Camping* (working title), © 2012 Carole Smith. Used by permission. You can contact Carole at www.pure-religion.com.

7 From a manuscript in process, *Pure Grace: Living on the Free Side of the Cross* (working title), © 2012 Brent Lokker. Used by permission. Brent has also written *Daddy, You Love Me: Living in the Approval of Your Heavenly Father.* You can contact Brent at www.brentlokkerministries.com.

8 Ibid.

the copy that you place on the back cover of your book. The content should be a summary or the main point of what your entire book is about.

3. Below is an example of what the map looked like for my book. If I were to write a book proposal for this book, I would include exactly what you see below. Your map should look similar.

4. Print out the one or two pages and put them up where you can see them (replacing the others you've put up).

Write Your Book
A Step-by-Step Guide to Write and Publish a Great Nonfiction Book

Introduction[1]
Others want to learn from your expertise and experience. Maybe only your family and a few friends will read your book. Maybe it will be a best seller. If you invest the time, this book will give you the guidance you need to prepare, write, and share your nonfiction book. Anyone can write—you can write—and it's time to write your book.

Chapter 1: How to Write a Great Book
The way you write a great book is to prepare a great book. Following the proven steps in this book will make the process more efficient and more enjoyable for you, and your end product will be an exceptional experience for your readers.

Chapter 2: Anyone Can Write
Among many voices speaking today, yours has its place. Using reliable tools, you can write a book that others will want to read.

Chapter 3: Questions to Ask Before You Begin
Knowing the answers to these questions will help your voice to be heard by the right audience with clarity, passion, and purpose.

Chapter 4: Get the Map
Writing with clear purpose, focus, and organization is a sure way to have readers follow you past your first chapter.

---

1   Note: I ended up not having an introduction, but when creating my map, I tried to write the elevator pitch as if it would go on the back cover of the book, which can be a summary of what the reader will get out of the book.

Chapter 5: Write Inspired and Write with God

Writing with inspiration brings to life information and experience that others can enter into themselves. If God has given you something to say, He wants to help you say it.

Chapter 6: Make Writing Efficient and Fun

There's a better way to write. Either rent a charming villa in the countryside, or use these twelve recommendations to maximize your energy and creativity.

Step 1: Prepare—A Map Will Get You There

Chapter 7: Prepare Step 1 – Create a Working Title and Subtitle

*"A great title will not sell a bad book, but a poor title will hide a good book from potential customers."
—Dan Poynter*

Chapter 8: Prepare Step 2 – Create Chapter Titles

The title of your chapter will set the tone for the chapter content that follows, so make a grand entrance.

Chapter 9: Prepare Step 3 – Develop an Elevator Pitch for Each Chapter

Each chapter's description is a tight pitch that identifies the purpose for the chapter with a clear, concise, and captivating description, inviting readers to invest their time in the chapter's content.

Chapter 10: Prepare Step 4 – Determine Your Section Headings

Creating smaller sections within each chapter gives the reader's eye a break from pages full of words and divides the content into bite-sized pieces for greater engagement and understanding.

Chapter 11: Prepare Step 5 – Align Your Book

Before you start writing your book, ensure it is properly aligned. Good alignment will ensure clear communication so that your audience can receive the many benefits your book can deliver.

Chapter 12: Prepare Step 5 – Set Up Your Manuscript Document

Focusing primarily on your content with minimal attention to formatting will get your book written more quickly. You'll also avoid extra costs later if someone doesn't have to undo all your formatting.

Step 2: Write—Live the Dream and Write Your Book

Chapter 13: Write Step 1 – Write Your Book Using Your Map
Many people dream of writing a book. If you're well prepared, writing can be an enjoyable and efficient process. Live your dream and write your book.

Chapter 14: Write Step 2 – Edit Your Chapters
The first draft is never your final draft. Once you've written the raw content of your book, the editing process you take to refine your book can make it stand out and shine.

Step 3: Share—Next Steps to Publishing

Chapter 15: Share Option 1 – Publish with a Traditional Publisher
Traditional publishers are valuable and can be an effective way to share your book with a wide audience.

Chapter 16: Share Option 2 – Do It Yourself
Now more than ever, easy-to-use tools are available to publish and print your book yourself.

Chapter 17: Share Option 3 – Get Some Help from Others
If you want your book to compete in the marketplace, get some help publishing your book. Choose your assistants wisely so that you invest your time and money well.

Chapter 18: Whatever You Do, Finish Your Book
If you have something to say, then prepare it, write it, and share it with the audience you have right now. Who knows … another book might be just around the corner.

Appendices

CHAPTER 10

Prepare Step 4:

Determine Your Section Headings

Creating smaller sections within each chapter gives the reader's eye a break from pages full of words and divides the content into bite-sized pieces for greater engagement and understanding.

What do you do when you see one huge block of text? Maybe it's an e-mail from a friend or colleague. Maybe it's an article on the Internet or a blog. Maybe it's in a book you recently started, and after looking at the opening two pages of a chapter you're wondering if you're going to make it to the end.

Take a look at your favorite newspaper, online news service, or blog site and count how many sentences there are in each paragraph. You'll probably find one to four sentences per paragraph. I suppose this says something about our attention span or how much we scan to consume more information in a shorter time, but I'm amazed how quickly readers will move on if they can't quickly determine what you chapter is about or if it *looks* too complicated.

The same is true for many sentences in one large paragraph or many paragraphs without a break. Maybe you were taught in school that paragraphs separate groups of thoughts. It is true that when the idea shifts, a paragraph break is needed. But paragraph breaks can also be used simply to break up a huge block of text that may be difficult to look at and read.

Many nonfiction books use *headings* to group blocks of related paragraphs throughout a chapter to help separate the chapter's content into bite-sized pieces and also give the reader's eye a break from pages of constant text. The idea is similar to what translators did with the Bible by adding section headings to organize and divide the original text into smaller sections.

So the goal of this chapter is to determine—before you start to write the main body text—what those core parts of your chapter are going to be and give those parts headings or titles. These divisions will define how you are going to support the one central point of each chapter. Ideally they will transfer directly into the book itself and become the headings of groups of paragraphs within each chapter. So you're not just writing words to map a structure; you're writing words that will most likely show up in your book.

Let's look at those sections.

Your Sections Within Each Chapter

Every book is structured differently because every author is different. Chapters within the same book can also be structured differently based on the needs of that chapter. Some may require additional sections or another level of sections. Divide your chapter how you see fit, but always consider what's going to make sense to the reader.

Regardless of how you structure your chapter, include the following three main parts in each chapter, with an optional but recommended fourth:

1. **Introduction into the chapter.** I like to encourage writers to "set the table" for their readers as they enter each chapter. Don't just jump into your main content.

   When guests come to your home to have dinner, you don't show up at the door with their portion of food in your hand, ready to shove it into their mouths. You welcome them to your home, engage in light conversation, ask if they'd like something to drink, etc.

   Your introduction doesn't have to be super long. Maybe it'll be only a few sentences. But it does need to say hello and "set the table" for your readers in some way to prepare them for what you're about to say to them.

   For example, in this chapter, instead of immediately telling you how to determine all your paragraph headings, I first chose to create the need for these divisions in your mind so you see that they have value. I tried to help you feel what your readers might feel if you chose not to break up your text in some way. This was my way of setting the table for this chapter.

   Different ways you can introduce each chapter may include:

   - **Review the main points of the previous chapter** (if desired and appropriate for your content). Many people don't read a nonfiction book through in one sitting. They read a chapter or two at a time. So it doesn't hurt to summarize the key point from the previous chapter since it may have been a few days since they read it. This also helps to connect previous content to what they're about to read.

     It's my opinion that a reader should never be confused about what you are saying or feel lost in any way (unless your book is just not for that person). The opening of a chapter is a great place to make sure all is in order, to help the reader see the big picture about what you're doing in the book and where you're headed, and to make your reader feel connected to the content and to you as the author. Consider the beginning of each chapter as another important place to make a good first impression.

- **A story or experience that embodies the central point of your chapter.** Speakers can get away with telling a joke or an irrelevant story as an icebreaker before they speak. That doesn't work so well in a book because the reader is expecting everything you say to be connected to the content. If there's no connection, it doesn't make sense.

  Telling a story that furthers your main point is very helpful, especially for readers who appreciate *showing* more than *telling*. As you're writing your book, be aware of stories you see in the media or from other resources. Using trusted sources outside yourself that further your point also gives you and your topic additional credibility.

- **Statistics or facts of some kind.** At the beginning of chapter 6 I cited statistics to demonstrate how quickly first impressions happen. You were probably aware that making a good first impression is important, so my introduction into chapter 6 just heightened your awareness a bit more. Statistics are a fantastic way to do this.

  Statistics can also be used to try to change a person's thinking by demonstrating facts or research that go against common thought. In chapter 1 of *What Your Dreams Are Telling You*, Cindy McGill and I provide evidence that everyone dreams every night.[1] It's a scientific fact. The reason we did this is that many people think they don't dream at all since they don't remember their dreams after they wake up. There are also some who don't believe God speaks to people through dreams today like He did in the Bible. The statistics (and the stories we also included) were our way of trying to shift readers' thinking to see that they are receiving messages at night as they sleep and it's a good idea to pay attention.

- **Other ways to relate the content to a felt need of the reader.** As you open your chapter, create a need for the chapter in some way. The reader picked up your book for some reason. How you introduce each chapter and make it relevant will determine whether the person continues to read your book and recommends it to friends or puts it back on the shelf to collect dust.

2. **Section headings throughout the chapter.** Write five to ten headings that encompass what the main content of your chapter will be.

---

1 See *What Your Dreams Are Telling You: Unlocking Solutions While You Sleep*, by Cindy McGill with David Sluka, published by Chosen Books in 2013.

(You can have more or less than that, but if each heading represents about 500 words, your chapter will be from 2,500 to 5,000 words, which is about average for a typical nonfiction book. Note: If you're going to write your book through blogging, each of these section headings can be a blog post. Five hundred or fewer words is a good length for a blog post.)

These headings are short phrases that capture the essence of the paragraphs that come after the heading. For this chapter I have five section headings that made it into the final form of this book: Your Sections Within Each Chapter, The Format of Your Outline, Example 1, Example 2, and Example 3. Under each of these heading came the paragraphs that supported these headings.

My original outline also included an introduction heading, which was to demonstrate the importance of breaking down your content. But usually you don't include a heading right at the start of your chapter since it's so close to the chapter title, so I didn't include a heading in the final version of the text.

Note that these headings are not just for your outline but should be transferred into the book to better organize your paragraphs for your readers. So be creative, have fun, and write them as if they are going to appear in the book … since they are!

Some approaches for headings include:

- Short phrases that summarize or set up the content to be read
- Action words or phrases
- Headlines like newspaper articles

Overall, it's good to keep these fairly short so they don't run to the next line. It's common to capitalize the first letter of each key word in the phrase, but not words like *of, at, in, to, with, the*, etc.

3. **Conclusion to the chapter.** This includes a summary of the main idea you have been trying to communicate and a transition to the next chapter. Sometimes the content will naturally flow from one chapter to the next and little to no transition is needed. (Notice that I did not include a conclusion in this chapter.) But often readers need you to build a bridge between the chapter they've just read to where you are taking them as they go into the next chapter. You don't need to do a lot. You can build a bridge with only a sentence or two. Just make sure your readers don't fall off the cliff and wonder where they are as they start the next chapter. Connect the dots and make the picture clear.

4. **Optional but recommended: Application of some kind.** For this book I've added a Your Assignment feature at the end of each chapter to help readers know exactly what the takeaway action is from each chapter. Depending on your book, you can include reflection questions, a summary of main points, study questions for personal reflection or group discussion, a closing prayer or meditation if the content is spiritual, action steps, takeaways, or whatever you think will help the reader take what you've shared and apply it.

I'm not sure the world needs more information. Anyone can use an Internet search engine and get the answers to most everything. I do think we need inspiration, deeper connection, customized application, and personal transaction to bring about desired change in our lives. With your book, inform, explain, and teach. But beyond these, help your readers make a transaction of some kind that will bring about personal transformation.

The Format of Your Outline—Your Chapter Map

Below is the format I recommend you follow as you write the section headings in your chapters. If you've completed Your Assignment at the end of each chapter, you have one or two pieces of paper with your book's working title and subtitle, and all your chapter titles with their respective descriptions. You will insert your section headings after each chapter's elevator pitch.

Here is a model of what each chapter map should include:

The chapter title

The chapter description/elevator pitch

The section headings, or the main points of your chapter, which should include:

- Introduction into the chapter—how you say hello
- Main body headings (as many as are needed)

  - Optional additional sub-points (as many as are needed for this and the other headings)

- Conclusion of the chapter—how you say good-bye and transition to the next chapter

Chapter Map Example 1

The first example is from _What Your Dreams Are Telling You: Unlocking Solutions While You Sleep_, published by Chosen Books.[1] Before the author and I started writing this book, we blocked out what each chapter would look like, similar to what I'm having you do with your book. You can see the following elements in the graphic below:

1. Chapter title
2. Chapter description
3. Section headings throughout the chapter (Some of the headings did not end up in the book exactly as we wrote them initially, but they still identified the main sections.)
4. Sub-points under the section headings that helped to build out the content further (the bullet points). These are optional, but I'd highly recommend building out your map to this level if possible. It will speed up the writing process later and will minimize or completely eliminate any writer's block.

    Important: The number of sub-points doesn't mean how many paragraphs you'll have in that section. They only capture the main ideas you want to communicate under that section heading. You will divide your content into as many paragraphs as needed to make your point. In the example below, it took two paragraphs to tell the story of how the sewing machine was invented. But we only needed to write one bullet in our outline to direct us to tell that story.

5. A line break after each heading and sub-point, which will be where you will start to write the main content of your book just a few days from now. I'm going to ask that you print out your complete outline at the end of this chapter, so for the sake of space, you may not want to add the line break until you're ready to write your content. I have _not_ added an extra line break below.

Chapter 1: Results When You Listen

Everyone dreams several times each night. Throughout history dreams have inspired inventions, songs, and poetry; warned of danger; and provided insight and direction. It's time to pay attention to this extraordinary source to unlock solutions while you sleep.

---

1   Cindy McGill and David Sluka, _What Your Dreams are Telling You: Unlocking Solutions While You Sleep_ (Bloomington, MN: Chosen Books, a division of Baker Publishing Group, 2013).

Introduction: Julie Gilbert Newrai's dream and $4.4 billion success story at Best Buy

Statistics that show everyone dreams every night

Dreams that have led to significant discoveries

- Sewing machine
- Theory of chemical structure
- Discovery of insulin
- Nerve impulses
- Optical computers

Other dreams throughout history

- Sitting Bull's victory at Little Big Horn
- Abraham Lincoln's dream of his murder
- Freedom for slaves—Harriet Tubman
- Sinking of the Titanic
- Nike brand name
- Paul McCartney tune "Yesterday"

Main takeaway summary: You are dreaming. Pay attention.

We ended up swapping out and adding a few things, but we basically followed our map all the way through. The chapter length is about 3,000 words.

Chapter Map Example 2

The second example is the outline of a chapter from the book <u>Culture of Revival: Perseverance with Joy (Vol. 1)</u>. Sean Feucht[2] and Andy Byrd,[3] along with a number of other international leaders, each wrote a chapter in this book on the importance of perseverance. Brian Brennt's chapter outline is below.[4] You will notice that Brian added some sub-points to his main points. The chapter length turned out to be about 3,000 words.

---

2   Contact Sean at <u>www.seanfeucht.com</u>. You can purchase this book <u>here</u> at Amazon.com.

3   Contact Andy at <u>www.andybyrd.com</u>.

4   Brian Brennt is a catalytic voice to youth movements across the nation. Used by permission. Contact Brian at <u>salvationencounter@gmail.com</u>.

The Unoffendable Heart

The culture of an unoffendable heart is one of the greatest joys you could ever have. It will not always be easy to maintain, but being motivated by what Jesus has done for you will give you the strength to arise and live with a tenderized heart before Him.

Introduction: Christy's dream about sitting in the game show called "Insult."

Indicator One: Dwelling on your Offense

- Repeating conversations in your head
- Shouting in the shower about someone who offended me

Indicator Two: Avoiding the Person who Offended You

- Who are you avoiding and why?

Indicator Three: Being Critical of the Person who Offended You

- Job 16:4–5 (NLT)
- The signs of a critical spirit
- How to get back on track
- Scriptures: Proverbs 17:9; Matthew 7:1–2; 7:3–5; Luke 6:37; Romans 14:10–13; 15:1; Galatians 6:1–4; Colossians 3:13–14; James 2:12–13

Indicator Four: Becoming a Diagnostic Expert on How Everyone Should Live Their Lives

- Example when I visited a church "discerning" everything
- Scriptures: Psalm 18:27 (NLT); 25:9; Proverbs 8:13; 11:2

Creating a Lifestyle of Grace

- Statements/prayers of grace for others
- Scriptures: Ecclesiastes 7:8–10 (NASB); Ephesians 4:32 (NASB)
- Forgiveness is not easy, but no matter what, I'm going to forgive

Conclusion: Specific prayers and a guide to help people identify where they've been hurt; forgive; renounce their anger, unforgiveness, etc.; and how to replace thoughts of bitterness when they come.

Chapter Map Example 3

The last example of a chapter map is from Amy Sollars,[1] also from *Culture of Revival, Vol. 1*. Amy's chapter mostly tells her story and at the end shares principles that have helped her.

Below you'll see her chapter title, her chapter summary, how she introduced her chapter, the main headings throughout her chapter, and how she concluded her chapter. Her chapter length is about 3,900 words, making each of her sections about 400 words.

---

1   Amy Sollars is one of the founders of the Fire and Fragrance and Circuit Rider schools. Amy travels and ministers all over the world with YWAM and other ministries. Used by permission. Contact her at www.amysollars. com.

This is what your chapter map should look like if you don't want to include sub-points.

To Those Who Overcome

The testimony of my life is that I have overcome. The ultimate reward of overcoming is encountering Christ Himself. When we know that our identity is found in the revelation of Jesus, His kingdom comes to earth and anything in Him becomes possible.

Introduction: The story of the first time I heard God's voice in the wilderness of Alaska

The early days

The battle for my soul

Jesus the Great Deliverer

Everyday journey of freedom

A new gift and its mistaken identity

Jesus, my identity

Friendship, accountability, victory

Keys to victory and the overcoming lifestyle

Spiritual and practical keys for encountering Jesus

Conclusion: When we choose Jesus and truth, we discover freedom in our identity in Christ and will overcome the lies of the enemy.

Your Assignment

1. Open your word-processing document.
2. Go to the chapter you want to work on first.
3. Each of your chapters should already have the chapter title and its corresponding description. Write as many section headings as need to build out your chapter map. Remember to build in how you'll set up and wrap up your chapter. Look back at the examples in this chapter as needed or follow the format below:
   - **Introduction into the chapter.** How are you going to set up your chapter for your readers?
   - **Section headings—as many as are needed.** How are you going to divide up your chapter's many paragraphs so that readers can easily follow what you're trying to say?
   - **Optional but super helpful: additional sub-points**—as many as are needed for this and the other section headings. Remember that one sub-point doesn't mean one paragraph. Sub-points only capture the main ideas you want to

communicate under each section heading. You will use as many paragraphs as needed to make your point.

- **Conclusion.** How will you wrap up your chapter for your readers and transition into the next?

4. Do the same for each of your chapters.

5. When you're done, print out a hard copy and put it up. You now have a working rough draft of the map to write your book. Congratulations!

6. Take a day off and celebrate! Seriously. Do something special to celebrate this success. If your spouse or significant other asks you why, tell him or her that the book you're reading recommends it. You've done something spectacular and it's good to take a breather before diving into the next chapter, which will refine your outline before you start to write the main content of your book.

CHAPTER 11

Prepare Step 5:

Align Your Book

Before you start writing your book, verify it is properly aligned. Good alignment will ensure clear communication so that your audience can receive the many benefits your book can deliver.

When a vehicle is not properly aligned, unnecessary stress is placed on other parts of the vehicle. If your book is not aligned, you will stress out your readers, leaving them wondering what point you're making or where they are in the scope of the book. Clear alignment keeps the reader informed and engaged.

One more analogy to drive home the importance of alignment. One of my chiropractor friends once told me, "Chiropractic is not about the back. It's about the connection—restoring or maintaining proper connection in the brain and spinal cord by removing interference to that connection caused by emotional, chemical, and physical stress."[1]

Writing a book is really not about the *content*. It's about the *connection* you make with the reader through your content. If your content doesn't connect, if your content doesn't communicate, you won't have readers. Good alignment reduces interferences to communication so that your readers don't have to work hard to enjoy your book.

This chapter is about ensuring the map you've outlined for your book is aligned so that you maintain good communication and a proper connection with your readers throughout your book.

If you've already written your manuscript (without an outline) and are using this chapter to see if your manuscript is ready to go to the editor, I recommend that you create an outline from your manuscript and then go through the six-point alignment check. Follow the instructions in Appendix C to do this.

---

1 Taken from material Dr. Lance Zimney and I worked on for his practice in Colorado. Connect with Dr. Lance at www.life2thefull.com.

Six-Point Book Alignment Check

Consider book alignment to be like the graphic below. The graphic includes only two chapters as an example, but these principles should be applied to all the chapters in your book.

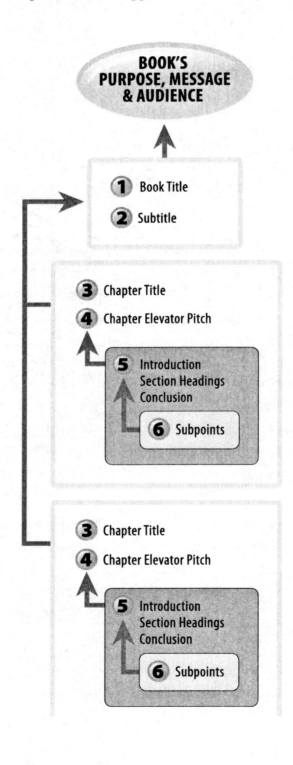

Let's review each part of book alignment. The numbers below correspond with the numbers on the graphic above.

To align the broader scope of your book:

1. Your **book's title** must align with the purpose and message of your book and the needs of your readers.

2. Your **subtitle** must align with the title, explaining it further and concisely explaining the benefit potential readers will receive by reading your book.

3. Each **chapter title** must align with your title and subtitle, breaking down your book into logical, organized sections.

4. Each chapter's **elevator pitch** must align with and clearly describe that chapter title. It articulates the one main idea of your chapter and tells why that chapter matters to the reader.

To align the content within each chapter of your book:

5. Each **section heading** must align with and support the chapter's elevator pitch and title. This is where breakdowns often occur—accidentally putting some content in one chapter that belongs in another or repeating content in more than one chapter that should be stated only once in one chapter. Take your time and properly align each section heading to its chapter elevator pitch and title. If it doesn't align, move it or delete it.

6. If you added **additional sub-points** to build out your outline's section content further, each sub-point must align with and support its section heading. If it doesn't align, move it or delete it. Each sub-point represents as many paragraphs as it takes to make that point. I know I've said this before, but I really encourage you to build out your outline to this level, which should eliminate any potential writer's block.

It's important to make sure each part of your outline is aligned with its higher-level part. I often run across books where some parts of the chapter don't really belong, which means (using this alignment model) that one of the sub-points (number 6) didn't align with its section heading (number 5), or one of the section headings (number 5) didn't align with its elevator pitch and chapter title (numbers 3 and 4). Number 6 must align with 5, which must align with 4, which must align with 3, which must align with 2, which must align with 1.

Your assignment for this chapter is to make sure everything is in its right place. Once it is, you're ready to write your book!

Your Assignment

1. If you haven't done so already, print out the outline you've created. Don't try to review all that you have written on a computer screen. Lay out the pages side by side on a desk or table so you can view your entire book at a glance.

2. Align the broader scope of your book.

    a. Review your title and subtitle and ask, **Do they align with the purpose of my book, the message I want to portray, and the needs of my audience?**

    b. Review each chapter title and ask, **Does each align with, submit to, and support my book's title and subtitle? Is there anything to add, delete, or change?**

    c. Review each chapter's elevator pitch one chapter at a time. Ask, **Does it clearly state the one main idea of this chapter and connect to the needs of my readers?**

    d. For each of the above, move things around, add, delete, and make changes as necessary until you are at least 90 percent sure your content is aligned and the way you want to present it in the book. You can do this on your computer or with a pen on the hard copy.

3. Align the content within each chapter of your book.

    a. Review the section headings in your first chapter and ask, **Does each align with and clearly support the one main idea of this chapter? Is there anything to add, delete, or change?** On the hard copy or in your computer document, move things around, add, delete, and make changes as necessary until you are at least 90 percent sure your content is aligned and the way you want to present it in the book.

    b. Review the sub-points under the section headings in your first chapter and ask, **Does each align with and clearly support the section headings? Is there anything to add, delete, or change?** On the hard copy or in your computer document, move things around, add, delete, and make changes as necessary until you are at least 90 percent sure your content is aligned and the way you want to present it in the book.

    c. Do the same for the section headings and sub-points for the other chapters in your book.

4. Use this time to make creative edits to your chapter titles, chapter descriptions, and paragraph headings as needed. It's worth the extra effort to polish things up

since the chapter titles and descriptions will be part of your table of contents, and your paragraph headings will appear throughout your chapters, dividing your paragraphs into easy-to-read sections.

5. Print out your revised outline and put it up where you can see it.

6. If you think one more pass of refinement is needed, take a break for a day or two and then repeat steps 2, 3, 4, and 5. You should be feeling pretty good right now and excited about what you've accomplished.

If you're a perfectionist, resist the temptation to refine your outline again and again and again and again. Sometimes your editing is not making things better; it's just saying them a different way. Things will change some once you start to write, so focus on getting the parts of your map as *complete* as possible, not *perfectly worded*.

Remember that many people try to write a book without an outline, so you're already ahead of the game in a big way. You now have a solid map in place that will guide you as you write and ensure your end product is all that it can be.

CHAPTER 12

Prepare Step 6:

Set Up Your Manuscript Document

Focusing primarily on your content with minimal attention to formatting will get your book written more quickly. You'll also avoid extra costs later when someone has to undo all your formatting.

This is your last step before you write your book. Inhale … exhale … and look at the great work you've done. You've built an awesome skeleton structure to support your content; now it's time to add everything else so your book will come alive.

Seven Steps to Set Up Your Document

The following steps will help you to set up your word-processing document so that all you need to do is write your content in the right place within the document. It's *super* time-consuming to undo line breaks, extra spacing, and formatting. So if you have an appreciation for saving time and money, the following steps will help you to do just that.

In the document that contains your outline, do the following:

1. **Use one word-processing document for your book.** Some people like to have a separate document for each chapter or to break up their books into different files. This is extremely inefficient and you'll end up combining them all at the end anyway. Keep everything in one document.

2. **Format your document.**

    a. Set one-inch margins all around.

    b. Insert page numbers in the footer. Go to Insert > Page Numbers. You don't need to do anything fancy. Select the options to center them in the footer.

    c. Set a half-inch indent on the first line of every paragraph (Format > Paragraph). Do *not* hit the return key an extra time between paragraphs.

    d. Set your line spacing as double space (Format > Paragraph).

    e. Use Times New Roman 12-point or similar font for everything.

f.   Don't do any other formatting on your manuscript. If you need to see your book formatted as you go, consider purchasing a design template from www. bookdesigntemplates.com. Otherwise, resist the urge to try to make your manuscript look like the layout of a book while you're writing it.

3. **Eliminate any unnecessary line breaks or formatting.** My guess is that you have at least three pages of written content for your complete outline. It should look like the examples I've provided in earlier chapters. The text should flow from page to page with limited formatting and without extra line breaks. If you hit the return key a few extra times to make the outline look a certain way on the page, remove those extra line breaks. That may mean that some parts of your outline that you want to stay together will end up on separate pages. That's okay.

4. **Add additional sections.** Add any of the following that you want to include in your book. Follow the order below and fill in the gaps as needed.

Title and subtitle (Insert them into your document. They should be at the top of page 1 and the first thing you see when you open your document.)

Copyright page (I'll explain in the next chapter what you need to put on this page.)

Endorsements

Dedication

Acknowledgments (Sometimes these are at the back of the book.)

Table of Contents (or just **Contents**)

Foreword (if you plan to have someone you know write one for you)

Preface

Introduction

Your chapter outline goes here, from chapter 1 through your last chapter.

Appendices (If you have more than one, list them as **Appendix A**, **Appendix B**, etc.)

Endnotes (I see endnotes more often than footnotes, which means that necessary and proper documentation of sources comes at the end of the chapter or book instead of at the bottom of the page where the quotes exist.)

Resources (This can include a bibliography of the resources you used in the writing of your book that you want to recognize and refer to your readers. This can also be helpful resources you recommend.)

Acknowledgements (Many authors put acknowledgments at the back of the book instead of the front. It's your choice.)

About the Author (information about you, usually longer and more detail than what you place on the back cover of your book)

Index (Word-processing programs have this function if you want to figure it out, but it is often something you hire someone to do for you.)

Promotional Ads/Materials or Other Books/Products (anything you want to promote)

5. **Make a second copy of your outline** within the same document. To do this, select your entire outline (everything that you have in your document right now). In Word or Pages, go to Edit > Select All. Copy the text (Edit > Copy) and then paste it (Edit > Paste) below the first outline so that you have two outlines. The first outline will serve as your map so that you can see at a glance the scope of your book for reference. It will later become your table of contents. (You will delete the section headings and sub-points at that time, but keep them in for now.) You will use the second outline that you just copied and pasted to write your book.

6. **Insert one page break after each section.** Between the two outlines (the first and its duplicate), insert a page break by going to Insert > Break > Page Break. Do the same thing after your title and subtitle, the copyright page, endorsements, dedication, table of contents, after the content of each chapter's outline, appendices, endnotes, etc. When you are done with this step, you will have inserted all of the page breaks that you will need during the writing of your book. Please resist the urge to hit the return key on your computer multiple times to get your pages to look the way you want … unless you're okay with doing the extra work to remove them later.

7. **Save your document with a file name in this format:** Your Title year.month. day. This format isn't necessary; it's just how I organize my files and versions of the same book. For my book, my file name today is Write Your Book 2013.10.02. docx (Word automatically adds .docx at the end). If you choose to save different versions, especially during the editing process, just change the day and the files will line up chronologically in your folder.

Your Assignment

1. Reread the tips in chapters 5 and 6.
2. Set up your document using the seven steps in this chapter.
3. Take a deep breath. Smile. You are ready to write!

Step 2: Write

Live the Dream and Write Your Book

I'm still puzzled when I hear an author speak, and then read his or her writing and the tones sound completely different. The first is usually friendly, relaxed, and conversational; the second typically formal, stiff, and academic. I'm amazed at how sitting in a chair in front of a computer can formalize a person's writing style.

Isaac Asimov, American writer and professor of biochemistry, once wrote to a young Carl Sagan. (It's impossible to describe Sagan in a few short words. Basically, he was a super-smart scientific pioneer who received many awards and honors, published more than six hundred scientific papers and articles, and wrote more than twenty books.)

Asimov told Sagan, "You are my idea of a good writer because you have an unmannered style, and when I read what you write, I hear you talking."[1]

I do not mention this quote to condone Carl Sagan's beliefs, especially those about God, but only to say that if someone as intelligent and academic as Sagan can communicate naturally in his writing, you can too.

Let readers hear you talking as they read the words in your book.

It's time to write.

---

1 Maria Popova, "Isaac Asimov's Fan Mail to Young Carl Sagan," blog post quoting *Yours, Isaac Asimov: A Life in Letters*, edited by Stanley Asimov. www.brainpickings.org/index.php/2013/07/22/isaac-asimov-carl-sagan-letters/.

CHAPTER 13

Write Step 1: Write Your Book Using Your Map

Many people dream of writing a book. If you're well prepared, writing can be an enjoyable and efficient process. Live your dream and write your book.

In chapters five and six I wrote about how to write inspired and write with God and how to make your writing efficient and fun. I recommend reviewing the tips contained in those chapters to get you in the mindset for writing.

These tips are not rules you have to try to follow. But they are a way to posture yourself toward writing that will release creativity and maximize your energy. Feel free to take a moment right now to review those tips and take any needed action before moving on to the rest of this chapter.

* * * *

If this is your first book, a lot of what you'll be learning in this chapter is *how* you write and what works best for you. Seth Godin says:

> The biggest takeaway for anyone seeking to write is this: don't go looking for the way other authors do their work. You won't find many who are consistent enough to copy, and there are enough variations in approach that it's obvious that it's not like hitting home runs or swinging a golf club. There isn't a standard approach, there's only what works for you (and what <u>doesn't</u>).[1]

Find what works for you and do it.

Five Ways You Can Write Your Book

There are a number of ways you can get your book onto paper. The first three approaches below involve speaking your content and then transcribing it into written form, which usually keeps the writing style relaxed and conversational—like you're talking directly to your reader over coffee.

---

1   Seth Godin, "Q&A: The writing process," blog entry posted July 22, 2013. <u>www.sethgodin.typepad.com/</u> <u>seths_blog/2013/07/qa.html</u>.

This is a fantastic approach to get your content about 75 percent done simply by sharing it with others. It can be especially helpful for anyone who comes alive in front of an audience. Having people around can bring out the best in a person and provide a live environment that is more inspirational than sitting in front of a computer.

The final two approaches involve writing for a blog or just to complete the book using your outline. Consider any or a combination of the following:

1. **Speak your book into a digital recorder** and get it transcribed. Speak your content, following your outline, using a digital voice recorder. Newer computers have this function built into the operating system. (For Apple products, hit the fn key twice.)

2. **Tell your book to a small group of trusted friends.** Gather a few people who want to know your story in more detail and share it with them, using your outline as a guide. Explain what you are doing ahead of time so you don't feel awkward sticking to the outline. This approach works well for someone who is writing his or her biography or telling stories of past events. Cover the information as it is presented in your outline. Then ask if anyone has questions. This can be very helpful to fill in gaps of information others may want to know but you didn't think of.

3. **Give a seminar or preach a sermon series,** using your book outline.

   - Be sure each session is recorded, that the quality is good enough to understand, and that you get a copy. You may want to record it yourself using a small digital recorder.

   - Each chapter represents one talk. So you will have as many sessions as you have chapters in your book.

   - Having CDs or DVDs of these sessions is a fantastic bonus, either to sell along with the book or to use as free giveaways during book promotion.

   - Transcribe your talks yourself or hire someone to do it. The Internet has many sources for transcription. I also give some recommendations on my website on the Resources page.[1]

4. **Blog your book.** A great way to write your book and develop your platform at the same time is to turn each section heading into one blog post. I recommend keeping each section under five hundred words so your post remains under five hundred words. So if your chapter is about four thousand words, you'll have eight blog posts for that chapter. If you want to know more about how to do this, check

---

1   www.david-sluka.com/resources.

out <u>How to Blog a Book</u>[2] by Nina Amir or her amazing <u>How to Blog a Book blog</u>.[3] Michael Hyatt's *Platform* also has very helpful and practical instructions about how to start or restart a blog.

5. **Write your book using your outline,** following the tips in chapters 5 and 6 and the nine steps below.

Nine Steps to Write Each Chapter

No matter how you're going to write your chapter (whether you speak it, blog it, write it, or record it), follow these steps:

1. **Pick a chapter.** For continuity's sake, it may help to write your chapters in consecutive order. However, if your outline is what it needs to be and you remain disciplined to follow it, it will create natural boundaries for you to stay within. I recommend beginning with the chapter you feel will be the easiest to write or the one you are most passionate about.

2. **Go to the first point you have written in your outline** for the chapter you have chosen. Set the stage for your chapter with a story, statistics, or another relevant way to connect with your reader. Insert a space after the header **and freewrite until you've said what you want to say.** Don't self-edit at this point. In other words, don't hit backspace. Just get what comes to mind on paper as fast as you can, as if you were having a conversation with a friend about your topic.

3. When you are done, **move to the next section heading your outline. Turn it into a heading** in the text by capitalizing the primary words of the phrase, and make it bold.

4. Hit enter so you go to the next line. Then **freewrite what comes to mind** about that heading topic, dividing the content as needed into separate paragraphs.

5. When you're done, **go to the next heading.**

6. **Repeat steps 3–5** until you're done with all the headings in your outline for that chapter.

7. **Make sure to wrap up your chapter in some way**—a summary of your one main point and a transition to the next chapter.

8. *Quickly* **write any extras you want to include** at the end of your chapter (takeaways, questions for reflection, steps of application, etc.). Don't spend too

---

2   Nina Amir, How to Blog a Book: Write, Publish, and Promote Your Work One Post at a Time. <u>http://www.amazon.com/How-Blog-Book-Publish-Promote/dp/1599635402</u>.

3   <u>www.howtoblogabook.com</u>.

much time on them at this moment, but get something down while the chapter is fresh in your mind.

9. **Ensure there is a section break or a page break after your chapter** before you begin the next one. (This should already be in place if you followed my suggestion in the previous chapter.) *Never* use the return key to get your content to the next page. Either you or someone else will have to do something with every keystroke you make. So make them wisely.

Repeat these nine steps for each of your chapters. By following these steps to write—not edit—your chapters, you will write your book much faster than if you try to write and edit at the same time. Get what only you can get down on paper; then go back and clean things up or have someone do the editing for you.

How Long Should My Chapter Be?

I recommend that you don't shoot for a specific chapter length unless you are under instructions from a publisher to hit a particular word count. Each chapter's map should contain all the content needed to make that chapter complete. By going from heading to heading, saying what you need to say for each, you should naturally have everything that is needed to complete the chapter. Focus on the content and let the length take care of itself.

So how long should a chapter be? As long as it needs to be. If you stay focused and organized and you end up with too much content, you can always refine it. If you have too little content, you can go deeper and build out the content more completely. But either way, your content remains focused and organized, which will engage the reader more than if you are just writing for length.

Nine Technical Aspects of Writing Your Book

As you write, here are a few technical issues to keep in mind.

1. **Write the content without distraction or delay.** Consider perfectionism your enemy. Don't try to wordsmith. Get your thoughts on paper as if you were telling them spontaneously to a friend. Avoid getting caught in the details of trying to make your first draft your final draft.

2. **Keep the formatting of your manuscript simple** (see additional tips in chapter 6). If you are concerned about the formatting and plan to publish your book entirely yourself, purchase or set up a template ahead of time.[1]

The purpose of the font and the formatting is to make your content readable. The font is not an expression of your personality or your brand. Use a common font

---

1 See www.bookdesigntemplates.com to purchase book design templates for Microsoft Word.

to *write* your book. If you or someone else is going to format your book, it will be simple and fast to change the fonts for *publishing* your book. Any professional who formats your book will not use Word, so anything you do will have to be redone or, in some cases, undone.

So keep it simple. Use a common serif font (like Times New Roman) for the text and a sans serif font (like Arial) for titles and headers if you want a variation from the body text.

3. **Use the tools that are a part of your word-processing program,** like centering text or creating page breaks. Someone will have to do something with every keystroke you make. Don't tab or use the space bar to center something or hit the return key to get to the next page. If you want to double-space your text, format your paragraph for double spacing (Format > Paragraph in Word or Pages) instead of creating extra line breaks that you'll have to remove later.

4. **Avoid long paragraphs**. The eye can only process so much text at the same time. One large block of text is like someone talking to you without taking a breath. Let your content breathe. If you have only one or two paragraphs on a page, insert a few more paragraph divisions.

    Paragraph divisions do not necessarily mean a change of topic; they can simply break up the content so it's easier to process. The strongest places in a paragraph are the beginning and the end. So if you have a sentence that you really want your reader to notice and you're not going to create a text callout (the boxes of text or pullout quotes that some books have), end the paragraph after that sentence so it doesn't get lost in the middle of the paragraph.

    If you're writing for a blog, web copy is often one to three sentences or one to four lines of text. You don't have to do that for a book, but people who read online often expect a similar format from books. Keep your paragraphs to bite-sized pieces.

5. **Hit the space bar only once after a period.** Search "spaces after a period" on the Internet and you'll find a passionate discussion about this issue.[2] *The Chicago Manual of Style* and MLA both recommend one space between sentences. Not hitting the space bar twice is a tough habit to break, but I recommend it. If you can't or don't want to break the habit, Microsoft Word's Find-and-Replace function is a quick way to replace two spaces with one. (From the toolbar go to Edit > Find).

6. **For emphasize and expression:**

---

2   www.theworldsgreatestbook.com/how-many-spaces-after-a-period/

- As a general rule, **do not put words in ALL CAPS**. Anything in all caps is considered shouting.

- **Use bold only for headers, titles, steps, or stages** you want to highlight in the text for clear reference and visibility.

- **Use italics to emphasize individual words or phrases.** It's a common practice, and it makes the point sufficiently.

- **Avoid having large blocks of text in italics.** The purpose of text in a book is readability, and a large block of italicized text is more difficult to read. Some older books have all Scripture quotations in italics. I do not recommend this.

- **Use exclamation points sparingly**. Overusing the exclamation point is like the little boy who cried wolf. It becomes annoying and you stop listening to it after a while.

7. **Respect the copyright of others** and **gather resource information** for footnotes/endnotes **as you go along** (see appendix D), including the page numbers of physical books. It is *super* painful to try to track down copyright information for quoting or referencing others' resources *after* you've written a chapter. Don't let this process interrupt a creative flow you may be in, but at a minimum, insert a footnote in the text as a placeholder (not manually, but using the tools in your word-processing program; e.g., Insert > Footnote).

   If you are using the Bible as a resource, you need to document which version you are using *after each quote*. Writers often use multiple versions within one book, and it can be a real challenge to determine which quote is from what version after the manuscript is done. Keep a running list of the translations you are using as you write. (Be aware that each version of the Bible has its own "fair use" parameters. Some allow for a certain number of verses to be quoted, as long as the quoted material does not constitute a certain percentage of the total work, without obtaining written permission. Some Bible versions have no limits; other Bible versions have no allowance for fair use and permission must be obtained from the publisher to quote even one verse.)

8. **Gain permission to use content** as you go. (See appendix E for the definition of "fair use" and how to obtain permission if needed.) It's a downer to hope to use another's content in your book, have them not give you permission, and then have to recreate that part of the book.

9. **If you quote from a source, quote accurately the first time, all the time.** Whenever you can, copy and paste from the Internet instead of trying to manually

type out the content from a handheld source. This lessens the chance of you making an error.

This is especially important for authors writing on spiritual topics, where they quote versions of the Bible or other scriptural texts. If you adjust the text in any way, you must show that.

For another point of view on technical issues to consider as you write your book, see Joel Friedlander's "9 Book Design Tips that Authors Need to Know," which complements what I've shared here.[1]

Extras to Write

Depending on what you want to include in your book, you may have other content to write besides the main core of your book. Below I've included possible extras (some usually included, like a copyright page, and others as needed, like appendices) and how to write them.

1. **Copyright page.** There are a number of things you can include on this page, such as the year of copyright, the owner of the copyright, reservation of rights and permissions guidelines, your contact information, and design credits. Look at a few books on your bookshelf for information you may want to include. Joel Friedlander has a good article about what to include here.[2] At the very minimum you need the following:

   Copyright © Year Your Name as the Owner of the Copyright

   If you used Scripture quotations in your book, also required here is the official copyright notice for whatever Bible version(s) you have quoted from. You can find this information in the front of the Bible you are using or at BibleGateway. com.

2. **Endorsements or Praise for Your Book.** The purpose of endorsements or praise for your book is to bring credibility to you as an author and to let others know that your book is worth reading. Many people try to get visible and respected leaders to endorse their books. A few things to keep in mind about getting endorsements:

   • People do read them. Some readers buy all of the books that their favorite leaders recommend. If you can get endorsements, they are good to have.

---

1   www.createspace.com/en/community/docs/DOC-1311.

2   www.thebookdesigner.com/2009/10/self-publishing-basics-the-copyright-page/.

- Not all of the people you want endorsements from will have time to read your entire book. You could ask these people for a character endorsement—to say something positive about you as a person, which will raise both your and your book's credibility.

- Know what purpose an endorsement would serve from each person you ask. Endorsements from sources who are not connected to each other are most helpful. Having five endorsements from the same small circle of influence doesn't broaden your audience.

- Some of the people you request an endorsement from may be in such a time crunch that they'll ask you to write it yourself. If you know the person well, you can write the endorsement they way you think he or she would. Then send it to that individual to review and tweak as needed.

- Endorsements don't have to be long. State clearly up front what you're looking for. Two to five sentences are sufficient.

- Endorsements don't have to come solely from "important" people that others recognize. Right now I have a best-selling book beside me with more than twenty endorsements on the first eight pages of the book. I recognize seven by name. I recognize another seven from the descriptions of who they are. While I don't know or care about the others, their endorsements still mean something simply by what they have to say about the book.

  Think about who you know and who might be willing to endorse your book. That might include leaders you know, people who have benefited from the content in your book, personal friends or colleagues. These people might also be potential marketing resources, so choose wisely whom you ask to read your book.

- Send out your book for endorsements only *after* you've completed the editing process and it is in the best shape it can be. Don't put someone in the tough place of having to say they can't endorse your book because it's not polished enough. Their names on your book represent a reflection on them personally and on their brand.

- Give a specific deadline of when you'd like the endorsement back. It's okay to follow up a few weeks before the deadline.

3. **Dedication**. Some authors choose to dedicate their books to a specific person or group of people. If others have been instrumental in your success or the content of your book, dedicate the book to them.

4. **Acknowledgements**. Acknowledgements are simply words of appreciation to specific people you'd like to thank. Some authors like to put these at the front of the book, others at the back.

5. **Table of Contents** or just **Contents.** These pages contain a summary of the contents of your book (chapter names and the pages on which they're found). I recommend also including short chapter descriptions in your table of contents. Look at some of your favorite nonfiction books for examples of how to design your table of contents.

6. **Foreword**. A foreword is a *word before* your book begins (watch the spelling of foreword; it's super embarrassing to spell it wrong). The purpose of a foreword is similar to the endorsements: to give you and your book additional credibility and raise the likelihood that someone will buy your book. Generally, you want a fairly recognizable person to write the foreword for your book.

   A foreword is a nice-to-have thing, but it is not mandatory. Sometimes a foreword may actually be unhelpful. In the book *What Your Dreams Are Telling You*, we chose not to have a foreword for the first printing. While we or the publisher could have asked a number of respected leaders for their endorsements, none of these leaders have influence in the specific audience we most want to reach. So until we have someone who can do that, we've chosen not to have a foreword.

7. **Preface and/or Introduction.** A preface and/or an introduction says what needs to be said before you get into the core content of your book. Sometimes they explain why you're writing your book. Or they may "set the table" so people have a base of knowledge before beginning your book. The contents of my first chapter are more like that of an introduction than a first chapter. Some people say that readers do not usually read the preface or introduction, but just jump to chapter 1. So keep in mind, only half of your audience may read your preface or introduction.

8. **Appendices.** An appendix contains information that you may not want to include in the body text of your book, but still want to include as a resource for your readers. I included a number of appendices in this book.

9. **Footnotes or Endnotes.** The difference between a footnote and an endnote is simply where you give credit to the resources you cite. A footnote appears at the bottom of the page where you cite the resource. Endnotes appear at the end of each chapter or at the end of the book.

   In general, books today seem to use endnotes more often than footnotes. Footnotes can clutter the page, and some writers prefer to list them all together at the end of the chapter or book. I usually recommend endnotes. I'm using footnotes in this book because I want readers to access the resource information quickly and not have to try to find the information on a different page. See Appendix D for what information to gather for your notes and how to format them.

10. **Resources.** Some authors choose to have a resources page that includes a bibliography of the resources used in the writing of the book. You can also use a resources page to identify helpful material you recommend for further study.

11. **About the Author.** This includes information about you as the author. It is usually longer and contains more detail than what is on the back cover of your book.

12. **Index.** Some authors choose to have a back-of-the-book index, which captures items of interest from the book (people, places, concepts, events) that the author believes the reader may want to find quickly. Word-processing programs have this function. But if you don't want to figure it out, you can hire someone to do for you for a few hundred dollars.

13. **Promotional Ads/Material or Other Books/Products.** If you have something you want to promote, consider some kind of an advertisement at the end of your book. This can include your blog or website, your services, speaking availability, conferences, seminars, or other resources.

Lead People to Yes or No

Earlier in this book I asked you, "Why are you writing your book?" I want you to consider that question again as you start to write the core content of your book.

What is the purpose of your book?

Is your purpose just to share the information you've gleaned, or do you want to inspire some kind of action? How are you going to connect the dots for your readers so they see a clear picture of who they can become and specifically what they can do to be different after reading your book?

From my days as a teacher and trainer, I found two downsides of communicating information:

1. *The audience writes off what you're saying because they think they've heard it before.* I've been guilty of this. Have you? Upon hearing a topic you think you know something about, you check out without trying to glean fresh insight.

2. *People hear or read information, and they equate inspiration with implementation.* There is a difference between *agreeing* with an inspirational concept in theory and *acting* upon it so the inspiration manifests itself in practical, profitable ways. I can count far too many times when I have come out of an inspirational experience feeling good, with great intentions for change, but wake up the next morning and quickly step into an old routine that gets me nowhere new.

I used to share the following graph at the start of my training sessions:

INSPIRATION   IMPLEMENTATION

Inspiration – Implementation = Self-deception   Implementation – Inspiration = limitation

Inspiration + Implementation = Acceleration

Inspiration minus practical implementation leads to self-deception—believing we have become something that we are not. A full head does not equal a big heart with serving hands.

But hey, don't knock inspiration too much, because inspiration is essential for growth. Implementation minus inspiration leads to limitation. We are limited to that which lies within us unless we allow the power and creativity of others to inspire us to more than what we can accomplish on our own.

When we combine inspiration with implementation, we accelerate our ability to grow.

My point? Inspire your readers, but help them to be more than just inspired. What do you want them to do with that inspiration? Help them grow.

Salespeople get a bad rap. But one thing they do well, if they're good at their job, is lead people to a decision. They ask for the sale and they close the sale. While working at Best Buy, I heard focus-group stories of customers who would come into the store with money in their pockets and the intent to buy something specific. But because the salesperson did not ask them to buy, they did not make a purchase.

People will read your book for a reason. What is that reason?

Your response to this question must be more than just sharing a good story or presenting intelligent, convincing information. You want to help people have thoughts and make decisions that will enable them to put what you present into practice in some tangible or measurable way.

How do you lead people to say yes or no? Clearly ask for a specific response. Let them clearly see whether they are saying yes or no. When working with business clients, I've watched employees and leaders use nonresponse as a successful way to imply agreement when they really don't have any plans of making changes. They listen, smile, and sometimes nod, but inside are not moving toward you in any way.

Let's not create an audience of hypocrites—people who think they are something they are not. You can't control the responses of others, but you can give them an excellent opportunity to make the best of your content.

People are picking your book up for a reason. Don't let them leave without getting the result they were hoping for when they first picked up your book.

Do more than just write your book. Lead people to a better place.

Ask for specific responses in your writing, whether that's through questions for reflection or application at the end of each chapter, steps or a guide to accomplish a goal, a challenge to think differently, a prayer … whatever fits your style.

Make your content count long past the time a reader closes your book.

Your Assignment

1.　Review Appendix B: My Writing Timeline. Make any necessary adjustments, then sit down with your calendar and create your writing schedule. It's better to make a plan and accomplish 50 percent of it than to not make a schedule and not have your book finished five years from now. Pencil in about two hours a day to write (or another length of time if something else works better for you). If you are going to take a writing retreat, create a plan for how and when you're going to write and what you want to accomplish.

2.　Depending on your book's content, it may be best to write the chapters in the order they appear in your table of contents. However, if you have energy around a particular chapter, write that one first. Your book map should be a safeguard to ensure the right information gets in the right place.

3.　Follow the Nine Steps to Write Each Chapter above for whatever writing approach you're going to take (e.g., speaking and transcribing, blogging, writing).

4.　If you find yourself in a rut for some reason, work on the part of the book that doesn't require original thought. For example, go back and read over what you've written so far and refine it. Sometimes that will kick-start your creativity and get you into a flow. Or go and do research for another chapter, work on the copyright page, consider how you can help your reader to apply your content, etc.

5.　Repeat steps 2 and 3 until you are done writing the first draft of your book.

CHAPTER 14

Write Step 2: Edit Your Book

The first draft is never your final draft. Once you've written the raw content
of your book, the editing process you take to refine your book can
make it stand out and shine.

Editing requires courage—courage to change or delete something that is good but not great. American author Annie Dillard says in her book *The Writing Life*:

> How many books do we read from which the writer lacked courage to tie off the umbilical cord? How many gifts do we open from which the writer neglected to remove the price tag? Is it pertinent, is it courteous, for us to learn what it cost the writer <u>personally</u>?[1]

In her uniquely eloquent style, Dillard exposes the fact that writers can get too attached to content that would be better eliminated for the sake of the reader. This is not easy.

This chapter is not an English lesson about how to find and fix all the technical errors like a proofreader would do. Only you can write the content. So I recommend focusing on refining your content as much as you can during the editing process outlined below and then let someone else catch anything you missed.

I strongly recommend finding a good proofreader who will align the technical aspects of your manuscript (its grammar, punctuation, usage, etc.) with *The Chicago Manual of Style*. I provide proofreader recommendations in chapter 17.

If you are a decent writer and you followed your outline well, you shouldn't have to pay for much more than a proofread. If a professional proofreader is out of your budget, find at least one friend who is good at English and is willing to help you out.

How to Edit Your Book

This process is similar to what you did in Chapter 11: Align Your Book.

---

1   "Annie Dillard on Writing," Maria Popova, <u>www.brainpickings.org/index.php/2013/08/09/</u> <u>annie-dillard-on-writing</u>.

After you have completed the first draft of your entire book, and *before* you send it to an editor or anyone else to read, **reread each chapter *out loud***. Take one chapter at a time. As you review each chapter, ask yourself these five questions:

1. **Does every section heading relate directly back to the chapter title and one main point of your chapter?** (This first question is to double-check that the alignment you had before you started to write your chapters has remained intact.) If not:

   - Refocus the heading or make a clearer connection between that section and the main point of the chapter
   - Put that section in a different chapter
   - Delete it.

2. **Does every paragraph in each section relate directly to the section heading?** If not:

   - Put it somewhere else where it fits better
   - Refocus it or make a clearer connection to that section's focus
   - Delete it

3. **How does the text sound when I read it out loud?** A conversational tone is very effective for most nonfiction. Does the text sound like a conversation you'd have with a friend? Reading your text out loud will expose areas that are not as fluid.

4. **Can I say what I'm saying more efficiently and effectively?**

   - If you can **say what you need to say with fewer words,** do it. It's easy to say the same thing over and over (albeit with different words) and not realize it. Land your point and move on.
   - Remember to **speak to the heart,** not just the head or hands. Emotions are God-given and play an important part in motivating a person to learn and act. As often as possible, help your readers *feel* what you are saying by using impactful stories and illustrations. Emotions are a natural fire that energizes change. Don't neglect them.
   - **Ensure your grammar, punctuation, and usage submit** to the bigger picture of understanding. Let me explain what I mean. Think of the last great concert you attended. Did you notice the sound technician? No, because everything he or she did was behind the scenes to make what was happening on stage come alive for the audience.

     The purpose of good grammar and punctuation is not to have a technically correct book. The purpose is to make your content come alive and make your message clearer, not get in the way of it. So if your writing is technically accurate but does not sing, make a change. Give your audience a great show, even if you break some technical rules in the process.

- **Use stories or examples** to connect the content to the reader even better. People often remember pictures more than principles. Bring your principles to life with memorable and relevant examples.

  - Note: If you use someone else's story—someone you know or from a published resource—be sure to get permissions if necessary and make proper documentation for endnotes.

- S**upport what you have said** with a reliable source to deepen your point and give your writing even more credibility.

  - Include all reference information for footnotes/endnotes.

  - As often as possible, take direct quotes from a source you can copy and paste. That eliminates your human error. For Bible references, include the abbreviation for the version you are using for *every* Scripture quotation somewhere near the quote unless you're using only one throughout your entire book. Also ensure you copy it exactly as it is written. Cutting and pasting from a website like www.biblegateway.com works well. You may need to touch it up a bit, like taking out superscript reference or verse numbers, but at least the words will be correct. You may add your own emphasis (italics, bold, brackets), but make it apparent that it is your emphasis or added words and not the Bible's by saying "emphasis mine" or "italics added."

5. **How can I best help readers apply the content** of this chapter? Consider including any or a combination of the following at the end of your chapter:

- Reflection or discussion questions
- Action steps
- Takeaways
- Closing prayer or meditation

Five Tips for Reviewing Your Editor's Feedback

If you have someone else edit or proofread your manuscript after you have gotten your content where you want it to be, here are a few tips to help you process the feedback you receive.

1. **Read it as a reader, not the writer.** If your editor has tracked changes that he or she suggests (in Word, Tools > Track Changes), select the option to show the "Final" version, not "Final Showing Markup." At this point it is important for

you to read your chapter as a reader would, not as the author. I also recommend reading it out loud. I find it helpful to hear how it sounds through my ears and not only in my head. It's much easier to hear when something is not flowing as it should.

2. **Focus solely on the content.** Avoid getting tripped up by how the text is presented or formatted. That will be taken care of after the manuscript is complete. Focus on the words since they are your words and only you can ensure you're saying what you want to say.

3. **Make changes as needed.** If you see anything along the way that you want to tweak, make those edits. But be sure "Track Changes" is turned on or you may end up paying for another full edit because your editor can't clearly see what you changed. Keep in mind that the purpose of this round of edits is not to make major changes (that should have been done before sending your manuscript to an editor) but to review the manuscript as a reader and tweak as needed.

4. **Look at your original manuscript** *only* if you run into a problem you cannot fix quickly by viewing "Final Showing Markup," "Original," or "Original Showing Markup." Editors work hard to make sure every change is for a specific purpose: to make the message more focused, organized, and powerful—not to lessen the impact of what you've written. But every once in a while they miss something. They misinterpret what you're trying to say or phrase it in a way that does not represent your voice. It's ultimately your responsibility to ensure that every word in your book represents you and your content accurately.

5. **Recognize and protect your voice.** Even the best proofreaders can cut deeper into your manuscript than what is appropriate. One of the authors I've worked with shared the following in an interview with me:

> Due to miscommunication with a proofreader, my manuscript was edited far deeper than was needed, which proved detrimental to my "voice." I've been insecure my whole life, so for me to have to stand up for my own literary voice was quite the experience. Instead of folding and saying, "Yes, yes, you're right," this was the first time that I said, "No, I know my voice." It was a great lesson in what my voice is. If nobody wants to read my voice, that's one thing. But I'm not going to change it to try to fit someone else's view. I'll try to be clearer and better, but I'm not going to change or dull my voice just because someone else doesn't approve.[1]

---

1 Interview with Mark DuPré, August 6, 2013, author of *How to Act Like a Grown-up*. See www.howiwrite. org/markdupre for the complete interview. Used by permission.

As you review the edits of another person, discern the difference between the following:

a. **Clearly saying something better.** Make these changes.

b. **Saying something differently, but not better.** Avoid chasing your tail making changes that do not specifically improve the content. An inexperienced writer can easily fall into this trap.

c. **Saying your content differently than how you would say it yourself.** An editor's role is to help you say what you're trying to say better than you said it yourself. A good ghostwriter is able to take on the voice of the author for which he or she writes. Be aware of whether an editor is making you sound *better* or *different*. Sounding better is good; sounding different is not. Reject these changes or find a way to say it better but in your voice.

Edit Until It Shines

While writing takes a lot of effort and discipline, I think the editing process is often more difficult. Cutting out what feels like parts of your soul is a tough task. But you must do it if you want your book to go from good to great. When boxers step into the ring, they are lean and ready to go. Unless you trim (and in some cases slash) the excess, your book won't be ready for primetime. Do what it takes to get your book in shape to share with others.

If you start to get discouraged in the midst of the editing process, take a deep breath and remember that you're done with the most labor-intensive part of your book: your core manuscript.

See the bigger picture—the purpose of your book and the impact it will have on the reader. Focusing on that may help you to endure the refinement process.

Have the courage to cut out what is not essential so that readers can experience your content in its purest form. Gold found in a mine is valuable, but people don't wear unrefined gold for all to see. Your content without the heat of editing refinement may be valuable, but it's not yet ready to share with others.

Apply the heat and see a wonderful gem appear—your content in its final form.

Your Assignment

1. Review your book chapter by chapter using the How to Edit Your Book steps in this chapter.
2. After you have edited your manuscript completely, which means you have done as much as you can do, find a professional editor to proofread your manuscript. See the editorial resources I list in chapter 17.
3. When you get your manuscript back from your editor, go through the Five Tips for Reviewing Your Editor's Feedback.
4. Celebrate! You have done something many people aspire to but never complete. You've written your book!
5. Review the final section of this book, which will give you options for how to share your book with others.

Step 3: Share

Next Steps to Publishing

There are many ways to share what you have written. In the next three chapters we'll look at three:

- A traditional, royalty-based publisher
- Do it yourself for $0 with easy-to-use tools
- Do some yourself and also get some help

For most people, I recommend taking the third approach: do a bunch yourself but get some good help for a few critical pieces. I used to try to do everything myself but realized that my strengths shine the most when I can focus on specific tasks.

Only you can write your book. Focus on that. But then find some smart professionals who can do far better at certain tasks than what you could do for yourself.

The only caution when going this direction is to choose your partners wisely. There are some great companies that can help you self-publish. Unfortunately, there are also companies that make great promises and take your money, but will leave you disappointed.

The next three chapters will address each of these options so you can determine which is best for you. I've provided some links to online resources so you can do additional research if you want. I've tried to give you a good starting place with my recommendations, but feel free to look for more or different resources with a simple Internet search.

In chapter 1 I said that there are three tragedies in communication: someone who makes a lot of noise but has nothing to say, someone who has something to say but says it poorly, and someone who has something to say but doesn't say it.

Right now you're in category three: you have something to say, you've said it, but you haven't shared it yet. You've come this far and have done the hardest work—writing and editing your book. No matter which option you choose, be sure to share what you have written in some way.

CHAPTER 15

Share Option 1:

Publish with a Traditional Publisher

*Traditional publishers are valuable and can be an effective way
to share your book with a wide audience.*

The publishing dream I hear most is from people who want to walk into their favorite bookstore and find their books displayed prominently on a table near the entrance or in an end cap. Just having it on a shelf in the store would be nice.

The problem is, Barnes & Noble, the largest book retailer in the US, carries from 60,000 to 100,000 titles in their nearly 700 stores in 50 states. *If* your book happens to be among the 1 percent of those that get picked up by a traditional publisher, you'll have to count on luck or divine providence for anyone to even find your book unless it is prominently displayed *and* it has a snappy title *and* a hot cover—unless you have an audience who will go specifically to the store to buy your book.

How many people do you know who would drive to a bookstore in their state to buy your book if they knew it was for sale? Less than a hundred? A few hundred? A few thousand?

The truth is, you need to have a track record of significant sales or an audience of tens of thousands to turn the head of a bookstore buyer. Otherwise, it's just not a good business decision for them to make.

Steven Piersanti says, in "The 10 Awful Truths about Book Publishing," that "the average U.S. nonfiction book is now selling less than 250 copies per year and less than 3,000 copies over its lifetime."[1] And only 62 of 1,000 business books released in 2009 sold more than 5,000 copies, according to an analysis by the Codex Group.[2] Additionally, bookstore sales have fallen each year since 2007, according to the US Census Bureau.[3]

So even if your book does make it into a bookstore, odds are that you are not going to have the kind of visibility and sales you're hoping for.

---

1   Steven Piersanti, "The 10 Awful Truths about Book Publishing," March 6, 2012, http://www.bkpextranet.com/AuthorMaterials/10AwfulTruths.htm.

2   Ibid (New York Times, March 31, 2010).

3   Ibid (*Publishers Weekly*, February 20, 2012).

This is why you shouldn't write a book to try to make money or to get it into a bookstore. Write your book because you have something worthwhile to say.

Who gets to hear what you say after that is up to your hard work, the relationships you have and develop, and some divine favor on your project. Otherwise, even with a traditional publisher, only the people who know you or are part of your publisher's network will find out about your book.

So while this chapter is about some things you can do to pursue getting your book picked up by a traditional publisher, regardless of whether one of them says yes, you can live your dream of writing your book and sharing it with others.

Be careful not to put your dream in a box by measuring your success based on whether or not your book is picked up by a traditional publisher or shows up in a bookstore or online. What it means to be an author and sell books has far outgrown these measuring sticks.

Quick Overview of Publishing

A few online resources will get you up to speed quickly about the field of publishing a book. I recommend reviewing the following articles and related material these authors link to in their articles.

- Take a few minutes to read the excellent article "Advice to First-Time Authors" by Michael Hyatt, former CEO of Thomas Nelson Publishers.[1] It will quickly get you going in the right direction. Another great post to read is "Five Publishing Hurdles and How to Clear Them."[2] The blog comments that follow this post are also very educational.

- Read literary agent Rachelle Gardner's article "All the Publishing Information You Ever Wanted."[3]

- Read Jane Friedman's article "Start Here: How to Get Your Book Published."[4]

- Take thirty minutes to look through the many fantastic articles in Chuck Sambuchino's Guide to Literary Agents Blog for instruction and information on literary agents, literary agencies, query letters, submissions, publishing, author platform, book marketing, and more.[5] On this blog page you can also search all of these categories to find other articles of interest. Just find "Search Categories" and select your category of interest.

---

1   www.michaelhyatt.com/advice-to-first-time-authors.html.

2   www.michaelhyatt.com/five-publishing-hurdles-and-how-to-clear-them.html.

3   www.rachellegardner.com/2013/05/all-the-publishing-information-you-ever-wanted/.

4   www.janefriedman.com/2012/01/28/start-here-how-to-get-your-book-published/.

5   www.writersdigest.com/editor-blogs/guide-to-literary-agents.

Research a Good Match

The good news is that publishers are actively looking for great manuscripts from authors who have a message others want to hear, and who already have an audience and are moving forward to share their message with others. If you want to find a publisher to work with, my first recommendation is to do some research about who is out there and who might want to publish your book. You don't have to spend hours and hours doing this. Try just one hour. The time will pass quickly.

Whenever I do even a little research, I'm amazed at the smaller niche publishers I find who have been in business for years, successfully publishing and selling for happy authors and profitable titles.

There are plenty of stories out there of authors who have been—for lack of a better word—screwed by publishing companies, and just as many publishing companies who've had to work with "challenging"—to say it politely—authors. Finding the right match is a dance, with both sides looking for a compatible partner. After all, you will represent them and they will represent you.

So do your research, think deeply and consider carefully who can best represent you, your DNA, and your message long-term. And then look at yourself from the publisher's point of view to see how good of a match you are for them, and how you and your book could enhance their product line.

Here are a few ideas about how to research a potential publisher:

- Invest an hour on the Internet, looking for publishers who may be interested in your title. For your search, type in the category or market of your book plus the word "publisher." For example, you might search for "business books publisher," "inspirational books publisher," "Christian books publisher," "cookbooks publisher," "self-help books publisher," "children's books publisher," or whatever category your book fits into. The first few pages of search results should display a variety of traditional, royalty-based publishers. Self-publishing companies will also show up, so discern who is who.

- Research books similar to yours and see who has published them.

- Find people who have published books. Buy them coffee and ask them what they did. If it's appropriate, ask if they can make a connection for you. Understand the position you're putting them in—putting their reputation on the line for you and your book. So leave an open door for them to say no, but still ask the question.

- If you are a Christian author looking for a Christian publisher, check out ChristianManuscriptSubmissions.com. I've found them to be a helpful resource. This site is a service of the Evangelical Christian Publishers Association, which has 260 member companies worldwide. This page[6] lists the top Christian publishers that would probably interest you. The site has a wealth of information and also

---

6   www.christianmanuscriptsubmissions.com/about_us.php.

provides instructions about how you can create and submit a proposal and find an agent.

- BowkerManuscriptSubmissions.com, which is "an online manuscript submission service for authors wanting to present their book proposals to the leading publishers in the industry,"[1] also has a list of publishers that are current subscribers to their service.[2] Bowker is the exclusive US ISBN and SAN agency.
- Jane Friedman has free market listings of publishers and agents here.[3]
- Preditors and Editors gives an extensive list of publishers they do and do not recommend. If you've found a publisher that looks interesting, dig a bit deeper and check them out here.[4]

Once you've found one or more publishers that interest you, follow the guidelines the publisher provides on their website to contact them and submit what they require.

Important: Traditional, royalty-based publishers and literary agents do not ask for money up front. If someone seems overly excited about your book and asks for up-front fees, ask more questions and proceed with caution.

Finding an Agent

While it's possible to get published without having an agent, most professionals recommend you find a good agent to represent you and your manuscript. Some excellent resources about what it means to have an agent, tips on how to find one, and lists of agents are below.

- Preditors and Editors gives a great summary of what it means to be represented by an agent. They also have a list of agents they do and do not recommend.[5]
- A great article by Chip MacGregor on "What you need to know before deciding on an agent."[6]
- A 14-minute video interview from Michael Hyatt with literary agent Rachelle Gardner.[7]
- Jane Friedman's market listings of agents.[8]

---

1   www.bowkermanuscriptsubmissions.com.

2   www.bowkermanuscriptsubmissions.com/about-us.php.

3   www.janefriedman.com/2011/09/26/free-market-listings/.

4   www.invirtuo.cc/prededitors/peba.htm.

5   www.invirtuo.cc/prededitors/pubagent.htm.

6   www.chipmacgregor.com/blog/agents/what-you-need-to-know-before-deciding-on-an-agent/.

7   www.michaelhyatt.com/an-interview-with-rachelle-gardner.html.

8   www.janefriedman.com/2011/09/26/free-market-listings/.

- The article "Finding a Literary Agent" by Ted Bowman.[9]
- Helpful information about finding and agent, along with a list of agents, at ChristianManuscriptSubmissions.com.[10]
- A list of literary agents who represent Christian authors from Michael Hyatt.[11]
- The article "How to Find an Agent" by Anna Genoese[12] or a PDF copy.[13]
- A thumbs-down list of agents from Writer Beware.[14] This is a great website for information on traditional publishing and self-publishing.
- Spend some time at Chuck Sambuchino's Guide to Literary Agents Blog.[15] His site has instructions and information on literary agents, literary agencies, query letters, submissions, and more.

Query Letters

A query letter is a short (less than one page, preferably less than half a page), well-crafted letter to an agent or publisher to get them interested in you and your book. Literary agent Andy Ross[16] says, "Chances are that most agents will spend about 10 seconds on your query deciding whether they want to follow up with you. Make sure those 10 seconds are used effectively, including finding the information she needs."[17]

The purpose of a query letter is to have them contact you. Below are excellent resources to help you start moving in the right direction.

- Read Andy Ross's "Nine Tips for Effective Query Letters" at WriteNonfictionNow. com.[18]
- Read "How to Write a Query Letter" by Rachelle Gardner.[19]

---

9   www.jcpublishers.net/page.php?68.

10   www.christianmanuscriptsubmissions.com/authors/agent.php.

11   www.michaelhyatt.com/literary-agents-who-represent-christian-authors.html.

12   www.annagenoese.com/article_series/demyst/free_articles/article_how_to_find_an_agent.html.

13   www.annagenoese.com/article_series/demyst/PDF/how_to_find_an_agent.pdf.

14   www.sfwa.org/other-resources/for-authors/writer-beware/thumbs-down-agency/.

15   www.writersdigest.com/editor-blogs/guide-to-literary-agents.

16   www.andyrossagency.com.

17   Andy Ross, "Nine Tips for Effective Query Letters," WriteNonfictionNow.com by Nina Amir, November 14, 2013, www.writenonfictionnow.com/nine-tips-for-effective-query-letters/.

18   www.writenonfictionnow.com/nine-tips-for-effective-query-letters/.

19   www.rachellegardner.com/how-to-write-a-query-letter/.

- Writer's Digest has an amazing summary about <u>The Query Letter</u> with an example and other resources.[1] Writer's Digest has a wealth of other articles <u>here</u> about queries as well as pretty much anything about publishing.[2] This is a must-see resource.

- <u>Jeff Riviera</u> has a great article about seven things to remember and include when writing a query letter.[3]

- Search "how to write a query letter" on the Internet and you'll find more than enough assistance to help you put your best foot forward. If you want to play in the big league, or even get the attention of "minor league" publishers, you need to write a big-league query letter. Do your research and write a great one.

Creating a Proposal

Acquisition editor and former literary agent W. Terry Whalin says, "90% of nonfiction books are sold from a book proposal. The majority of these books have not been written—but a proposal has been carefully crafted to catch the attention of a publisher."[4]

Publishers or agents don't want to see your manuscript. They want to see a proposal—a well-written, well-presented proposal.

If you've completed the "Your Assignment" sections in this book, you will have most if not all of the information you need for your book proposal. Each publisher or agent will ask for the information in a slightly different format.

When creating your proposal:

1. Find out what the publisher or agent is looking for and follow those instructions. Exactly. Provide everything they ask for and do not include what they say to leave out. Not following their specific instructions is a good way to disqualify yourself immediately.

2. Deliver an outstanding proposal in content and format. Present your proposal with the same level of excellence you would expect the publisher to have when publishing your book. Your proposal gives an agent or publisher a picture of who you are and your writing ability.

---

1 www.writersdigestshop.com/query-letter.

2 www.writersdigest.com/editor-blogs/guide-to-literary-agents/queries-and-synopses-and-proposals.

3 www.publishingbasics.com/2008/05/29/from-self-published-to-published-is-it-possible-to-land-a-top-agent-when-youve-self-published-or-published-independently/.

4 W. Terry Whalin, "How Do You Get a Nonfiction Book Published?" Right-Writing.com, accessed October 5, 2013, www.right-writing.com/published-nonfiction.html.

Below are some resources I recommend to help you create an outstanding book proposal to submit to an agent or publisher.

- I've personally used Michael Hyatt's PDF download <u>Writing a Winning Non-Fiction Book Proposal</u>. It's worth every cent of $19.97.[5]

- For $14.99 Nina Amir offers <u>The Easy-Schmeasy Nonfiction Book Proposal Template</u>, which is a short, downloadable Microsoft Word cut-and-paste template including helpful information about what to include in each proposal section.[6] Nina also provides individual consultations to answer questions about preparing a book proposal.

- A wonderful proposal template for Word is available to purchase and download from <u>Mike Larsen</u>[7] and Joel Friedlander <u>here</u>.[8] It includes nonfiction and fiction templates as well as Mike Larsen's 51-page PDF "Keys to Becoming a Successful Writer Faster and More Easily than Ever." Mike Larsen also does <u>nonfiction book proposal coaching</u> and can edit your proposal until it's ready for submission.[9]

- Literary agent Steve Laube includes guidelines and recommendations for nonfiction and fiction book proposals <u>here</u>[10] for free.

- You can find another free proposal template at <u>Ted Weinstein Literary Management</u>.[11]

Book Proposal Submissions to Publishers

You may also want to consider the following three paid services:

- For $99 <u>BowkerManuscriptSubmissions.com</u> will lead you through a process to fill out and submit a proposal for participating publishers to view. Your proposal remains in their database for six months.[12]

- For $98, you can submit a proposal to <u>ChristianManuscriptSubmissions.com</u>, and they will post your proposal for potential review by their member publishers. Your

---

5   www.michaelhyatt.com/writing-a-winning-book-proposal.

6   www.writenonfictionnow.com/landing/easy-schmeasy-book-proposal-template/.

7   www.larsenpomada.com.

8   www.bookdesigntemplates.com/proposal/.

9   www.larsenpomada.com/non-fiction-book-proposal-coaching/.

10   www.stevelaube.com/guidelines/.

11   www.twliterary.com/bookproposal.html.

12   www.bowkermanuscriptsubmissions.com/author/index.php.

proposal remains in their database for six months. They have a "Critique & Edit" service available for an extra fee.[1]

- For $99, The Writer's Edge Service offers a slightly different approach.[2] After you submit your proposal, their editors will evaluate it, and if it is among those they feel have merit, they will send it, along with others, in a monthly report to their participating publishers. If your proposal is not accepted, you will receive feedback about your proposal's strengths and weakness, with recommendations for improvements.

Networking

Networking is a fantastic way to open doors for you and your book. And you'd be surprised how many doors can open after one door does. Consider one or more of the following:

- Attend a writers' conference. Search "writers conference" on the Internet to find one that works for you. Two popular and reputable conferences are Writer's Digest Conference[3] and Author101 University.[4]

- Interact with other authors and industry professionals while taking online writing classes. Check out San Francisco Writers University for free and paid subscription classes.

- Reach out to others in your network. Let them know you're writing a book. You may find you have some knowledgeable friends you didn't know about.

- Join a writers' club. There are probably local chapters near where you live. If you are a Christian author, check out Christian Writers Guild led by *New York Times* best-selling author Jerry B. Jenkins.[5] They have some great conferences, courses, contests, and other helpful writing resources.

- Find authors who live in your area. Take them out for coffee or lunch and ask them to tell their stories. Listen and take notes.

- Start following other people's blogs and join the conversations by adding helpful comments. The goal is not to promote or sell your book, but rather to build relationships and do something for *that* blog. The good you do there will come

---

1   www.christianmanuscriptsubmissions.com/about_us.php.

2   www.writersedgeservice.com.

3   www.writersdigestconference.com.

4   www.author101university.com.

5   www.christianwritersguild.com.

back around in due time. If you're looking for some good blogs, start with this list of "100 Blogs You Need in Your Life" from LeavingWorkBehind.com.

- Write for someone else's blog. Peter Sandeen has a great list of guest-blogging sites.[6] Or inquire at websites, blogs, magazines, or news sources that may benefit from your content.

Costs

If an agent or publisher asks you for money, they are what some call a vanity or subsidy publisher. Depending on the contract and the author, traditional publishers may pay an advance upfront.

Profits

Authors who publish with traditional, royalty-based publishers usually receive 5 to 15 percent of the book's profits, which translates to about $1 per book. Read this great article about traditional publishing profits by Ted Bowman.[7]

This may not seem fair to you as an author. But in defense of the traditional publisher, I don't think it's wrong that they receive the bulk of the profits since they are absorbing all of the costs of the book—production, printing, distribution, promotion, etc.

If your book sells millions of copies, great! But most books sell fewer than 10,000 copies, even with a traditional publisher.

If you want to see real profits from your book, do your part in marketing it. Then your book (and hopefully subsequent books) will be profitable for you and your publisher.

Proofreading, Interior Design, Cover Design, Printing, Sales, Distribution, and Marketing

One of the great things about going with a traditional publisher is that they handle many of the details that can make the self-publishing process laborious. Your book's proofreading, interior design, typesetting, cover design, printing, sales, distribution, marketing, and more are taken care of by your publisher. You will be a part of most of these activities, but your publisher will take the primary lead and cover the costs.

How Long Does It Take?

One of the downsides to going with a traditional publisher is the amount of time it takes for your book to be made available—even after you've finished writing the manuscript. It's not that a

---

6   www.petersandeen.com/list-of-guest-blogging-sites.

7   www.jcpublishers.net/page.php?127.

publisher couldn't get your book done faster. But the systems, markets, catalogues, buyers, publicists, etc., that the publisher works with require long lead times to get your book ready for the public.

Once you sign a contract with a publisher, you're looking at about twelve to eighteen months before your book is out.

In the Meantime

If you are clearly set on publishing your manuscript with a traditional, royalty-based publisher, stay the course and don't give up. Stories abound about authors who were rejected dozens of times before receiving a contract. Believe in your message, receive wise counsel, and refine your manuscript while you wait. But persevere and find the right company to publish your book.

If you're not as certain about your publishing goals, read chapters 16 and 17 of this book and consider self-publishing. It is possible to land an agent and/or a publisher after you've self-published. I did that with <u>What Your Dreams Are Telling You</u> with Cindy McGill. Jeff Riviera wrote about his experience <u>here</u>.[1]

If you do land a traditional publisher, congratulations! As you work with that company, remember that this is a joint partnership that requires effort on your behalf to promote and sell your book. Do what it takes to be a great partner for your publisher and you'll find great success.

Your Assignment

- Walk into publishing educated. This will take a bit of time. Whatever you do, guard against getting overwhelmed by all the information that is available. If you're reading this chapter before you've started writing your manuscript, schedule thirty to sixty minutes every week, as you write your book, to learn more about the publishing business. Research the links I've included in each of the following sections in this chapter:
    - Quick Overview of Publishing
    - Research a Good Match
    - Finding an Agent
    - Query Letters
    - Creating a Proposal

---

1   <u>www.publishingbasics.com/2008/05/29/from-self-published-to-published-is-it-possible-to-land-a-top-agent-when-youve-self-published-or-published-independently/</u>.

- If you're going to pursue a traditional publisher or an agent, your first step is to determine who you want to write to, then send them a query letter. Take some time to research the links I've included so you can write an excellent query letter.

- If you're reading this chapter before you've started to write your book, chapters 1–11 and 13–14 will help you put together all that you need for your proposal. Generally, an agent or publisher asks for only a few chapters, so it is not necessary to write your entire book before reaching out to an agent or publisher. (This is true for nonfiction. But for fiction, publishers want an author to write the whole book, and polish it, before submitting a query.) Write the two chapters that you feel strongest about.

- Follow up on one recommendation from the Networking section in this chapter.

CHAPTER 16

Share Option 2: 8 Steps to Do It Yourself for $0

More than ever, easy-to-use tools are available to publish your book yourself.

The purpose of this chapter is to point you to some resources that will allow you to publish your book completely by yourself—making it available for others to purchase online—for $0.

While you can do this entirely on your own, I recommend that you get someone else involved, at least for the cover (see the next chapter for more information and resources).

You may also want to consider "crowdfunding" your book at Indiegogo—"the crowdfunding solution that empowers ideas and enables people to donate funds easily."1 Or check out Kickstarter. See Top 10 Crowdfunding Sites for Fundraising in *Forbes* for other online resources that can help you fund your book using crowdfunding.2 You can find a great article on *how* to crowdfund here.3

If you have absolutely no budget, I recommend the following. (If you search "self-publish" on the Internet, you'll find an overwhelming wealth of information on other options.)

Step 1: Build Your Platform

A physical platform is what a person stands on in a crowd so an audience can see him or her. For an author, your platform is how you connect with the people who want to hear what you have to say through a website, a blog, speaking engagements, webinars, book signings, social media like Facebook and Twitter, newsletters, e-blasts, videos, podcasts, etc. Your platform gives you a place to stand and share what you have written.

Very few people can be like Justin Bieber—just put a few videos on YouTube and a year later have one of the top songs in the country. But everyone's book has that chance. To give yours the best start, begin building your audience now.

---

1 From www.indiegogo.com/about/our-story.

2 Chance Barnett, "Top 10 Crowdfunding Sites for Fundraising," 5/08/2013, www.forbes.com/sites/chancebarnett/2013/05/08/top-10-crowdfunding-sites-for-fundraising/.

3 www.firepolemarketing.com/how-to-crowdfund/.

Early in this book I recommended that you purchase *Platform* by Michael Hyatt. But since this chapter is about what you can do for $0, go to Hyatt's website, which has a wealth of great information that you can access for free. Invest some time and do some reading, watching, and listening here.[1]

If you do nothing else, watch the 22-minute video on how you can Launch a Self-Hosted WordPress Blog in 20 Minutes or Less.[2] A self-hosted blog will cost you some money. So will www.squarespace.com. It's not free, but it is reasonable. And if you're serious about building a platform, it's a good way to go.

Just because you have a platform doesn't mean you'll have potential buyers for your book. The goal of a platform is to have a place where people can interact with you.

You can check out quality free blog and website options at www.weebly.com, www.blogger.com, www.wordpress.com, or www.tumblr.com/about. These are good options that will give you a place to begin and also provide the flexibility to expand in the future if needed. If you're not sure of the importance of an author website, take a look at both sides of the issue as presented by Jane Friedman here.[3]

Don't dismiss the importance of social media. Nearly one out of four people in the world are a part of a social network of some kind.[4] More than half of all Americans have a profile on a social networking site, and it's not just kids who are signing up. If you're over forty, you may not think social media is for you. But 55 percent of adults ages 45 to 54 are part of a social network.[5]

More people are connecting on social media than anywhere else. If you're not a part of that network, you are missing an amazing opportunity.

Maintaining and growing your platform is an ongoing process. You don't need to sign up for everything right away. Figure out what's most likely to work for you and do it well.

Step 2: Complete Your Manuscript

Follow the instructions in chapters 1–13 of this book to write your manuscript.

Step 3: Polish Your Manuscript

Follow the guidelines in chapter 14 to edit and proofread your book.

---

1   www.michaelhyatt.com/category/social-media.

2   www.michaelhyatt.com/ez-wordpress-setup.html.

3   www.janefriedman.com/2013/09/27/publishers-author-websites/.

4   "Social Networking Reaches Nearly One in Four Around the World," eMarketer, June 18, 2013, www.emarketer.com/Article/Social-Networking-Reaches-Nearly-One-Four-Around-World/1009976.

5   Jay Baer, "11 Shocking New Social Media Statistics in America," Convince&Convert.com, accessed October 25, 2013, www.convinceandconvert.com/the-social-habit/11-shocking-new-social-media-statistics-in-america/.

Almost everyone knows someone who's excessively fussy about details. If you've got a person like that in your life, he or she might be willing to proofread your book for free. It doesn't hurt to ask.

Another way to find areas you may need to improve on is to ask others for feedback. Be super specific about what you're looking for from each person. In the past, I've articulated very clear instructions to people who still did what they thought instead of what I asked for. Determine what kind of help you're looking for and consider what kind of feedback each person is qualified to give.

For example, you may want one person to look at the credibility of your content, another to check the flow of ideas, and another to focus on the technical aspects of your writing. If you're not specific with each of these people, you may get advice on where you need commas, a different font recommendation, or comments on your formatting.

Choose your reviewers wisely so you don't end up getting a variety of completely different ideas. In the next chapter I offer tips on how to process an editor's feedback, which will help you process and effectively use the responses you receive.

Do make sure to have someone else look at your manuscript. Little errors in a book (which you may not notice but others will) distract readers from your message. Not a good way to launch a book. Put your best foot forward and go the extra mile to present your content in the best way possible.

CreateSpace.com

CreateSpace has the best resources I've seen to publish a book completely on your own. They are an Amazon company, so they can get your book on Amazon.com for others to purchase. You can sign up for free at www.createspace.com.

The following steps will outline the CreateSpace process to publish your book free of charge.

Step 4: Design and Typeset the Inside of Your Book

If you're planning to publish only as an e-book (a popular approach), you can skip this step.

Here on CreateSpace.com you will find information about how to set up your Word document and how to design and format the content. There are also interior templates for a number of popular book sizes that you can download for free.[6]

Step 5: Design Your Book's Cover

CreateSpace has a free online tool called Cover Creator, which is accessible from your member dashboard once you set up an account with CreateSpace. They have an image gallery of more than 2,000 free images that you can use to create your cover. It's a great way to do a cover yourself, although I recommend that you get some help in this area.

---

6   www.createspace.com/Products/Book/InteriorPDF.jsp.

Another resource to create your cover (especially if you're only going to do an e-book) is www.myecovermaker.com. It's not free but is very reasonably priced—under $5.

If you must do the cover yourself, I recommend that you:

1. Read Area 4: Complete Cover Design in the next chapter. It'll give you some tips and insights for what to think about when designing your cover.

2. Go to your favorite bookstore or search online for some covers that are attractive to you. Your book's cover is more about your readers than it is about you, so try to look at your cover's design from their point of view.

3. Create a few cover possibilities and get some feedback from friends who will be honest with you. The section on Getting Feedback for Your Chapter in the next chapter will show you how to process the feedback you receive and ultimately choose the cover that's best for your book.

People will judge your book by its cover, so make it a good one. Consider including the following:

Front cover

- Title and subtitle.
- One primary image or background that shows visually what your book is about or what the end result will be for someone who reads your book. The primary image needs to be big enough and clear enough to be able to see in a thumbnail image online. So a bunch of small details won't do you much good. Making one clear point through your cover image or background is the best way to go. See the section in the next chapter on "How to Design Your Cover" for more discussion about this.
- Your name as the author.

Spine

- Book title (subtitle optional).
- Author name.
- If you have a logo of your company or ministry, you can put that on the spine similar to what a publisher would do.

Back cover

- A short phrase or sound bite for your book, usually at the top of the back cover.
- A summary or description of the book—your hottest, most engaging copy to sell a potential reader on your book.

- In some cases it's helpful to list some bullet points of what the reader will learn or gain from your book.
- Depending on space, you can include one or two *short* recommendations or praise for your book. You can put longer recommendations inside the book. Choose the best parts for the back cover.
- Author bio.
- Author picture, usually a head shot with a simple, non-distracting background.
- Leave space, per CreateSpace guidelines, for the bar code.

See the instructions on how to access the tool creator on CreateSpace.com here.1 You will need to sign up for CreateSpace and log in to your member dashboard to access the tool. If you own Adobe InDesign, CreateSpace has a tutorial on How to Create a Cover in Adobe InDesign.

What Not to Do with Your Cover

Common errors when creating a cover include:

- **Choosing an image that is dated, looks old-fashioned, or is overused**. How many times have you seen a cover with an image of a person with his hands raised in victory—usually on a mountaintop at sunset? It's a great image and it may express the sentiment of your book perfectly. But consider how you can communicate the same message with a different image.
- **Overcomplicating the design with too much clutter or layering too many images together**. Romance novels can get away with a collage of images. Nonfiction generally cannot. This kind of design does not leave potential buyers with a positive feeling or a clear picture of the benefits they will receive if they buy your book. Designer, colleague, and friend Yvonne Parks says, "People want to dive in and get lost in your book and not get stuck in a cover that feels like a hoarder's closet."2 At a quick glance, either in a bookstore, on a book table, or looking at a thumbnail online, your image should give a potential buyer a clear picture of the emotional benefit of your book.
- **Using standard or old fonts**. I've watched a cover shift from being average and common to outstanding and unique simply by changing the font. There are numerous fonts available. A few to avoid are Papyrus, Impact, and Comic Sans.

---

1   www.createspace.com/Tools/CoverCreator.jsp.

2   Yvonne Parks designed the cover of this book and is one of the primary cover designers I recommend to others. She is wonderfully talented, very focused and organized, has a track record of winning covers, and is easy to work with. Her website is www.pearcreative.ca.

- **Using too many fonts or a font that is difficult to read**. A good cover usually has one distinctive font and a secondary sub-font. The secondary font should be simple; otherwise, it will only create clutter. Yvonne has told me, "Font design is like fashion. Unless you're in the circus, you don't mix stripes, plaid, and checks." At a quick glance, either in a bookstore, on a book table, or at an online thumbnail, a potential buyer should be able to read your title quickly and easily.

- **How you use the font**. The placement and size of the title and other written elements on the front cover (subtitle, author name, foreword name, etc.) can take your cover from boring with a homemade look to interesting, unique, and professional. In the next chapter I show six designs that Yvonne presented to me for this book and reveal how I chose the one I did. You can see in those examples different ways Yvonne used fonts effectively.

Everything in your design must submit to one end goal: to communicate a clear message that will evoke the right emotion to attract the right audience. It may be a *great* cover, but if it doesn't accomplish this goal, it's not the *right* cover.

Step 6: Make Your Book Available Online for Print-on-Demand

CreateSpace will take you through the entire process to set up your book and make it available for sale online. This process is fairly self-explanatory and CreateSpace has good customer service if you need assistance. If you still need assistance, companies listed in the next chapter provide support to their authors and can help you make your book available.

People often have questions about book size, copyright, ISBNs and bar codes, royalties, costs to buy copies of their book, and how to set a good price for the book. I'll address each of these issues below.

Book Size

Two common sizes are 5.5 x 8.5 and 6 x 9. If you want to do something different, consider these options:

- Workbooks can be 8.5 x 11.
- One of my authors wrote a series of pocket devotionals that are 4.5 x 7.5.
- I recommended to one author that she size her book to 5 x 8 because it would have been a bit too thin at 5.5 x 8.5. We made the size a bit smaller, and typeset the inside text so it could breathe a bit more, and the book came out wonderfully. It feels like a "real" book and not a booklet, which is what we were trying to accomplish.

Copyright

Copyright means a person's *right* to *copy*. One of the most common questions and concerns I hear is "*How do I secure copyright for my book?*" Some authors seeking to work with me are extremely concerned that I or someone else may use or steal their work; therefore, they guard their writing with great intensity.

Copyright law states that copyright is secured when a work is created in tangible form. Once you write or type your first word on paper (or save the document on your computer), you have copyright protection against anyone who may try to take your content unjustly. Nothing else is required to secure copyright, although the Copyright Clearance Center recommends registration.[1]

For a more complete explanation of this issue, you'll find a fantastic summary of copyright basics along with some common myths at <u>Writer Beware</u>.[2] Additional information can be found at the <u>Copyright Clearance Center</u>,[3] or search "copyright" on the Internet.

Some people believe that no matter how hard they try, someone *will* pirate or steal what they've done, so the best thing to do is make the most of it. You can read about that perspective <u>here</u>.[4] I don't agree that literary theft is inevitable, but I do like the recommendations Fred Gleeck makes about how to market your information better.

ISBN and Bar Code

ISBN stands for International Standard Book Number. It's the unique identification number for your book. If you use CreateSpace, they can assign your book an ISBN at no cost. You retain all rights and maintain 100 percent control of your content. However, official records will say that "CreateSpace Independent Publishing Platform" is the publisher. The benefit of having a CreateSpace-assigned ISBN is that you have <u>expanded distribution options</u> to libraries and academic institutions.[5]

If you want to be classified as the publisher, you need to purchase your own ISBN. See the next chapter for how to do that.

A bar code is a small square box that contains machine-readable code of your ISBN and the price of your book. It is placed in the lower-right corner of the back cover of your book. When you create your book cover using a CreateSpace template, they will have you leave a blank space in this location so they can add a bar code there for you during the printing process.

---

1   "Obtaining Copyright Protection, Registration and Other Requirements," © 2013 Copyright Clearance Center, www.copyright.com/content/cc3/en/toolbar/education/get-the-facts/obtaining_copyright_protection.html.

2   www.sfwa.org/other-resources/for-authors/writer-beware/copyright/.

3   www.copyright.com/content/cc3/en/toolbar/education/get-the-facts.html.

4   www.publishingbasics.com/2010/06/30/why-the-obsession-to-protect-your-writing-is-misguided/.

5   www.createspace.com/Products/Book/ExpandedDistribution.jsp.

If you have someone else do your cover for you, the designer will need to leave that part of your back cover blank. There are instructions and templates your designer can use on CreateSpace. com.

Royalties and Percentage of Profit

CreateSpace's royalty information is here,[1] and they have a royalty calculator here,[2] where you can plug in your numbers to see how much profit you will receive depending on your book's trim size, interior type, and number of pages. The calculator also shows profits from books sold through Amazon Europe in Great Britain and continental Europe. Your profits will depend on the sales channel, a fixed charge, and a per-page charge.

To give you a quick example using royalties that Amazon is giving as of this publication, if your book is about 40,000 words, which translates to roughly 176 pages in a 5.5 x 8.5 paperback, and you sell it for $14.00 a copy, you will receive:

- $5.44 if sold on Amazon.com (about 38 percent).

- $8.24 if sold on CreateSpace's eStore (about 58 percent).

- $2.64 through their Expanded Distribution option (about 18 percent), which makes your book available to more online retailers (like Barnes & Noble), bookstores, libraries, academic institutions, and distributors within the United States.[3]

Buying Your Own Copies

This link will give you information about what it will cost to buy your own copies of your book through CreateSpace.[4]

For the scenario above (176 pages in a 5.5 x 8.5 paperback), you will pay $2.96 per book. If you want to purchase more than about 300 at one time, it's best to use another printer, because your cost per book will drop considerably. See the next chapter for printer recommendations.

A shipping calculator is available on CreateSpace.com, which enables you to calculate how much it will cost for the number of books you want to print.

---

1   www.createspace.com/Products/Book/.

2   www.createspace.com/Products/Book/#content6:royaltyCalculator.

3   www.createspace.com/Products/Book/ExpandedDistribution.jsp.

4   www.createspace.com/Products/Book/.

Setting Your Price

I believe the retail price reflects a book's value. A higher price (within reason) equals higher perceived value. Lower price, lower perceived value.

I thought for months about how I should price this book, which falls into the self-help genre. Do I price it lower and hope to sell more, making up for the lower price in volume (the Wal-Mart strategy)? Or do I price it higher and get only the customers who are serious about the book, possibly selling fewer copies but with a higher margin of profit?

I am 100 percent certain that my book will save writers *at least* $500 in editing costs. Probably more. My one-day Write-Your-Book workshops, where I walk participants through the steps in this book, are $297. So should I sell a paperback copy of this book for $13, or the e-book for $9.99, when it empowers people to fulfill their dream of writing a book, gain credibility through being published, and potentially make thousands of dollars through repeat sales?

I considered going with $29.97, but ended up pricing this book at $24.97 for the 8 x 10 paperback or the Kindle e-book. Through the program with Kindle Direct Publishing (KDP), whoever buys the paperback can get the Kindle e-book for free. At some point I may sell a PDF version of the book (the same thing I uploaded to CreateSpace.com to create the paperback) for $19.97 as a download from my website. The price can be lower because I will receive a higher margin since Amazon wouldn't be taking a cut.

So, how much is your book worth? This is a dangerous question, since many authors tend to rate their books too high or too low based on their level of self-confidence. If you're on the low side, may I just say that your book is worth buying. If you're on the high-confidence side, you're going to have to look at the market and see what your book is worth from your reader's perspective, not just your own.

There is such a wide range of nonfiction books available, it's tough to give you an average to shoot for. If you're a leader or speaker, your book will likely fall into the $12 to $30 range, depending on your area of expertise and your audience. Business books are generally priced higher (about $25) than religious, inspirational, or self-help (about $15). Instructional, academic books are priced even higher.

I recommend doing a little research at your local bookstore in your book's genre. You can also research online. Check out the retail price, not the discounted price Amazon or other retailers might use.

Don't price your book based on its length. A long book doesn't mean a higher price and a short book doesn't mean a lower price. I've purchased short hardcover business books for $24.99 and a 30-page PDF download for $30. Some curriculum is priced closer to $100. A tabletop collection of artwork printed in color sells for $49. Do some research and price your book by its value to your audience and what is comparable in the market.

Remember that *pricing* your book (choosing the price that will be printed on the back cover) and *selling* it are different. Price your book at what you feel is its value to your customer and what will sell in the market. Then do special promotions to sell your book at a lower price. CreateSpace and KDP allow you to change your price for special promotions. If you host seminars or if you're an itinerant speaker, state your book's value but offer special deals for those who "buy today." People like getting a deal, so price your book as it should be priced and then give your customers something special.

Dan Poynter has a great resource about <u>How to Price Your Book</u> if you want additional advice.[1]

Price and sell your book strategically and you'll find greater success.

Step 7: Convert Your File to E-Book Format and Make Available Online

For an outstanding list of e-book publishing resources, including free downloads, I highly recommend Jane Friedman's article "<u>How to Publish an E-Book: Resources for Authors</u>."[2]

About two years after introducing the Kindle, Amazon reported that customers were buying more e-books than all paperbacks and hardcovers combined.[3] E-books are an amazing way to make your book available to the public. Many authors choose to publish only an e-book and not a hard copy of their books. This eliminates the extra work of setting up the inside layout and formatting, which allows the author to publish more quickly.

Inside your CreateSpace account's setup for your paperback book, there is an option to upload your document to be a Kindle e-book. You can select that option or you can go straight to <u>kdp.amazon.com</u>.

Your Word document will need to be converted to e-book format. Kindle has a converter that can successfully convert your Word document if it is formatted properly. If not, you may have to pay a minimal fee to convert it. Instructions are on the KDP website.

There are other ways to convert your document to e-book format if you want to do it yourself, including free software at <u>www.calibre-ebook.com</u>. Apple's Pages program for Mac has an option to export your document to e-pub, which is a popular e-book format that works with every device and app except Amazon's Kindle.

There are several advantages to publishing with KDP:

- It's free to set up an account, publish your e-book, and make it available online.
- Kindle provides easy-to-follow resources to walk you through the process of building your book for Kindle, including preparing, formatting, and merchandising your e-book.

---

1   <u>www.parapublishing.com/sites/para/information/business.cfm#doc604</u>.

2   <u>www.janefriedman.com/2012/02/10/10-questions-epublishing/</u>.

3   <u>www.theguardian.com/books/2012/aug/06/amazon-kindle-ebook-sales-overtake-print</u>.

- Kindle Matchbook allows those who buy a hard copy of your book to purchase the e-book at a discount. Read a <u>blog</u> case study about the Matchbook program.[4]

- After you've published, you can make changes to your content at any time.

- You can publish in English, German, Spanish, French, Italian, Portuguese, and Japanese.

- The Kindle website is available in all of the above languages except Japanese.

- You can earn up to 70 percent royalties on your e-book.

- If you have everything in order, it takes less than 15 minutes to set up, and in 24 hours your book will be available online for purchase.

- If you enroll in <u>KDP Select</u> and publish exclusively with KDP, you can make your book available in the Kindle Owner's Lending Library, which allows Amazon Prime members to check out your e-book for free.[5] Based on how many times your e-book is checked out, you will receive a monthly financial reward.

- KDP Select's Promotion Manager tool allows you to give away free books worldwide for a limited period of time. This may not sound like something you want to do, but giving your book away will actually lead to selling more books.

I personally don't see a big downside to publishing solely with Kindle. The only objection is that the book will not be available in other e-stores, like iTunes and Barnes & Noble. However, the Kindle Reader app is available as a free download for every device (iPads, NOOKs, Android tablets, computers), so if people want your book, they can easily get it. And with all the incentives KDP gives you to publish solely with them, it's a win for everyone.

Everything you need to know about KDP can be found <u>here</u>.[6]

If you would prefer to publish in both the Kindle format and e-pub, which works on the NOOK (Barnes & Noble's e-reader device) and all other readers, check out <u>www.nookpress.com</u>.

Many people go with KDP and <u>Smashwords</u>. Smashwords is a free service where authors can convert their Word documents to e-books and distribute them to the most popular e-stores except the Kindle store. By formatting your book in both of these formats, you will cover almost all of the places that sell e-books. You earn 85 percent for books sold through Smashwords and 60 percent anywhere else. <u>Here</u> is a great blog on how to publish with Smashwords.[7]

---

4   <u>www.jetlaunch.net/amazon-matchbook-case-study/</u>.

5   <u>https://kdp.amazon.com/self-publishing/KDPSelect</u>.

6   <u>https://kdp.amazon.com/self-publishing/help</u>.

7   <u>http://blog.smashwords.com/2011/09/how-to-self-publish-ebook-with.html</u>.

For e-book conversion in mass quantities, you can upload e-book files to an online distribution service like Amazon's KDP. I've also used Digital Divide Data.[1] They recruit, train, and employ high school graduates from impoverished backgrounds in developing countries. I respect their mission and I've been very happy with the quality of their product and with their customer service. They provide many data services for reputable organizations, but online book distribution is what I've used them for.[2]

Setting Your E-Book Price

Most people think they should get an e-book for much less than a hard copy since they're not getting ink and paper, just an electronic file. However, the amount of work authors put into writing their books is exactly the same, regardless of what format the reader gets (paperback, hardback, PDF, e-pub, mobi, html, audio, etc.).

A common price for nonfiction e-books is $9.99. You can price it much lower with the hopes of selling more. Do some research on Amazon.com and see what e-books like yours are selling for.

For e-books, I still recommend pricing based on the book's value and what the market will allow, then doing some special promotions.

Step 8: Continue to Market

Once you've publishing your book and it's available online, here are a few ways to continue to market your book.

- **Consider making an audio book**. You've already done the hard part of writing your book. Through Amazon's Audiobook Creation Exchange (ACX), you can make it available for others to purchase from Amazon.com, audible.com, or iTunes.

- **Create a package**. If you're a leader or speaker, you probably have other resources you can bundle with your book: a PowerPoint presentation, an MP3 of a recent talk that is related to your book's topic, a study guide, 30 minutes of free consultation (if you want to promise that), your top ten tips for something (formatted into a nice-looking resource). Be creative and think of something you already have that you could bundle with your book. If you don't already have something, think about what you could put together quickly and inexpensively.

---

1   www.digitaldividedata.org/services/ebooks/.
2   www.digitaldividedata.org/services/.

- **Book-signing party**. When you launch your book, invite friends and others who may be interested to a book-release party. It'll probably cost you something to do this—at a minimum, refreshments, unless you can talk your friends into pitching in. Make it doable for you, but find a way to celebrate.

- **Run special promotions**. CreateSpace and Kindle Direct Publishing have options for running special deals. Check out those resources, then expand on them with ideas of your own.

- **Continue to build your platform**. A short, thin diving board doesn't have much stability or spring. It's the same way with what you have to stand on as you launch your book. Go deeper, longer, and wider in the way you build your platform—not just for this book, but for you as a person to share what you have. Review what I've shared about this in Step 1 of this chapter.

- **Provide excerpts from your book** on your blog, website, or other social media venues. CreateSpace and KDP provide the "Look Inside" feature for their books so potential buyers can get a taste of what they're buying. Since you own the content and the right to copy, you could provide a free PDF download of the first chapter or selected excerpts on your website. Reprint excerpts strategically in other places: your blog, a magazine, newspaper article, other people's websites. I've repurposed certain parts of this book for my blog—keeping the length under 500 words and choosing parts that would spark interest in potential buyers. Reach out to sources who may be interested in your content and pitch it to them. They'll usually be looking for something that matches their publication word count (online articles are often 500 to 900 words), so be ready to tweak and customize your content if asked.

- **Guest host**. Writing for other people's blogs is a great way to do something for someone else and give some exposure to you as a person and to your book(s). Peter Sandeen has a great <u>list of guest-blogging sites</u>.[3] You can also inquire at websites, blogs, magazines, or news sources that may benefit from your content. Freely give and you will usually freely receive.

You Can Do It

Publishing on your own will take some time. Even though I've been helping leaders and authors since 1995, putting some parts of this book together and building my own platform has required a steep learning curve.

3　<u>www.petersandeen.com/list-of-guest-blogging-sites</u>.

Writing a book is hard but simple. *Publishing* a book is hard and can be complicated, especially if you're not comfortable with technology. Accept that fact, learn what you need to know, and do it. You *can* do it. *You* can do it. It's worth it.

But if you don't want to, or would prefer investing your time in another area, get some help. See the next chapter for the assistance that's available for parts of the process you may not want to tackle on your own.

Your Assignment

1. Think about crowdfunding your book. A little more money toward your book will yield a more excellent product for you to share with others. Check out one of the crowdfunding websites I mentioned at the beginning of this chapter.

2. If you're not into crowdfunding, think of other ways that you may be able to raise some money to put toward this book. I've known authors who told others that they were writing a book and requested financial assistance to publish it. Since they could show that they had a good manuscript completed (or at least in the works), people they knew offered to help.

3. Follow steps 2 and 3 in this chapter to finish your manuscript.

4. Sign up for createspace.com.

5. Follow steps 4 through 7 to publish your book.

6. Consider how you may want to market your book through your platform or other methods.

7. When your book is published and available, celebrate! You are officially an author. Have a book-signing party to launch your book.

8. Continue to build your platform and market your book. And if you have more to say, think about writing your next book. (Sorry to bring this up so soon. You might need a rest at this point. If so, you'll start getting the itch to write more when it's time…or when people start asking for your next book.)

CHAPTER 17

Share Option 3: Get Some Help

If you want your book to compete in the marketplace, get some help
publishing your book. Choose your assistants wisely so that you
invest your time and money well.

Getting help with some essential pieces of the publishing process can ease the load on you as the author and be a worthy investment in the message you have spent time crafting into a book.

As I've compiled resources for this book, I've been reminded of how many really smart people there are doing great work on behalf of writers. Help is available within your budget. But like any service you pay for, you need to choose your assistants carefully.

In the exploding world of self-publishing, there are plenty of rip-offs you want to avoid. Preditors and Editors[1] and Writer Beware[2] are two great resources to make sure you're investing wisely.

I begin below with some companies than can help with the entire process of publishing your book. Unlike traditional, royalty-based publishers, these companies will charge you for their services.

After that you will find ten areas for which you can hire someone to make the book-publishing process easier:

1. Building your platform
2. Editing/proofreading
3. Interior design and typesetting
4. Cover design
5. Printing
6. Creating e-books
7. Creating audio books
8. Obtaining ISBNs and bar codes
9. Fulfillment and distribution
10. Marketing and networking

---

1   www.invirtuo.cc/prededitors/peba.htm.
2   www.writerbeware.com.

For each of these topics, I'll share what I think you should know, then identify some of the resources that have served me well. While these resources have been good for me, please search out what will be best for you.

Warning: This is a long chapter and it contains a lot of information. You may want to read only what applies to the area(s) where you want help. Or skim through the general information in each of the sections and then check the resources that interest you as you have time or need.

If you're planning to write more than one book, or will need similar services in the future, consider your research a trust-building process with people you'll probably work with on later projects.

Publishing your own book is a lot like running your own business as a sole proprietor: you do everything, or at least you have to know about everything. So take some time, educate yourself a little, and then decide what you'd prefer to do yourself and where you want assistance.

One-Stop-Shop Companies that Can Help You Self-Publish

Many companies claim to be able to do everything for you. Since this book is not paid advertisement for such companies, I'll just give you a general idea of what's out there.

Self-publishing resources are widely available and there are plenty of rip-offs in the self-publishing business to avoid. Check out Preditors and Editors[1] and Writer Beware[2] to make sure you're investing wisely. Ted Bowman of JC Publishers also has insightful articles about what goes on behind the scenes in the self-publishing world and offers many free helps for authors.[3]

Look closely at what companies promise so you don't get stuck with any of these undesirable results:

- Your manuscript does not receive the professional editing attention it needs to represent all that you want to say—without errors.

- Less-than-professional interior design and typesetting.

- Less-than-professional cover design or a cover design that you don't like.

- Marketing promises that sound like your book is going to be available in bookstores, when your book will actually only be in a catalog or computer system, alongside many other books, so it can be seen and ordered by a bookstore. Your book will only get into a bookstore if someone knows about your book and asks the manager to order it. A physical copy is not present in bookstores and no other marketing is done.

---

1   www.invirtuo.cc/prededitors/peba.htm.

2   www.writerbeware.com.

3   www.jcpublishers.net.

- Your name is next to the copyright date but you do not have full control of your book and you don't own your final files (inside and cover), so you can't take your book elsewhere.

For additional information on what true self-publishing is and what to watch out for, check out the following resources:

- Download a free e-book Publishing Basics by SelfPublishing.com. They also have helpful self-publishing educational resources on this page. Scroll down to see resources for publishing associations, educational programs, seminars, and conferences.[4]
- View the free Publishing Basics Seminars by Ron Pramschufer (self-publishing expert), Fred Gleeck (information marketer), Burke Allen (media strategist), and Bob Bly (copywriter and Internet marketing strategist).[5]
- Read Ted Bowman's helpful article "What is a True Self-Publishing Company."[6]
- See Johnathon Clifford's website www.vanitypublishing.info for helpful definitions, advice, and warnings about publishing, proofreading, and editing.

Self-Publishing Companies

Below are some resources that I and others I know have found reliable. I cannot guarantee you will have 100 percent success with any company, since every company has its strengths and weaknesses. Research carefully to find what the best fit for you. A good overview of issues you want to consider when choosing a company is here.[7]

- As of this book's printing in January 2014, SelfPublishing.com is the number-one self-publishing website on the Internet. It's a spectacular full-service resource to help you publish your book yourself by becoming your own publisher.[8]
- BelieversPress.com provides a *full* suite of professional publishing services for Christian authors.[9] A great resource.
- Respected industry professional Dan Poynter's ParaPublishing.com is extremely helpful.

---

4   www.selfpublishing.com/steps/step1.php.

5   www.publishingbasics.com/seminar/.

6   www.ezinearticles.com/?What-Is-a-True-Self-Publishing-Company?&id=7318703.

7   www.dogearpublishing.net/the-competition.php.

8   www.selfpublishing.com.

9   www.BelieversPress.com.

- <u>Mill City Press</u> has a number of <u>convenient publishing packages</u> to suit your needs, including services such as distribution and fulfillment. They also have an excellent royalty structure.
- <u>Xulon Press</u> is a popular self-publishing company for Christian authors.[1] They have a free publishing guide available on their website.
- <u>WestBow Press</u> helps authors self-publish all genres of books, but they specialize in books with Christian morals, inspirational themes, and family values.[2]
- <u>CrossBooks</u>, an imprint of B&H Publishing, a trade publishing division of Lifeway, can help you write, edit, market, and sell your book to your audience.[3]
- <u>Art Bookbindery</u> is a self-publishing company that will guide you through the entire process of preparing and printing your book professionally.[4]
- <u>Christian Writers Guild Publishing</u>, started by *New York Times* best-selling author Jerry B. Jenkins,[5] will help you gain "the skills to produce a polished manuscript by personally mentoring you through a six-month course called *Published.* Then we work with you to produce a finished book you can be proud of."[6] If you finish their course, they will publish your book.
- <u>MorganJamesPublishing.com</u> is known as the "entrepreneurial publisher," that actively works "with their authors to help them not only maximize revenue from their book royalties, but also build new business and increase their revenue substantially through follow-on sales to their readers."
- Four popular self-publishing, print-on-demand companies, each with their own variations, include:
  - <u>DogEarPublishing.net</u>. They have a full suite of services. They also provide a <u>comparison of the competition</u> (it leans toward DogEarPublishing, but it still gives a good overview of services you'll need).[7]
  - <u>Lulu.com</u>. Do what you want to do yourself and then <u>hire the professional services</u> you need.[8]

---

1   <u>www.xulonpress.com</u>.

2   <u>www.westbowpress.com</u>.

3   <u>www.crossbooks.com</u>

4   <u>www.artbookbindery.com</u>.

5   <u>www.cwgpublishing.com</u>.

6   "Why CWG Publishing?" Taken from the promotional materials on this page: <u>www.cwgpublishing.com/about-us/</u>.

7   <u>www.dogearpublishing.net/the-competition.php</u>.

8   <u>www.lulu.com/services/</u>.

- OutskirtsPress.com provides customized publishing packages and à la carte services. Get three free e-book publishing resources at their website.[9]

- This link on CreateSpace.com shows professional services for every step in the publishing process.[10]

Area 1: Building Your Platform

At the beginning of the previous chapter, I wrote that your platform is how you connect with the people who want to connect with you through contact points such as a website, a blog, e-mail list and campaigns, webinars, speaking engagements, book signings, seminars, conferences, social media like Facebook and Twitter, videos, podcasts, etc.

More than ever technology is playing a big part in maintaining and growing an audience. Nearly one out of four people in the *world* are a part of a social network of some kind.[11] That's about two billion people. As of 2013, more than 1.1 billion people around the world are on Facebook. Someone clicks the Facebook "Like" button more than 4.5 billion times a day. That's more than 52,000 times per second.

Over half of all North Americans have a profile on a social networking site, and it's not just kids who are signing up. Fifty-five percent of adults 45 to 54 are a part of a social network.[12]

More people are connecting on social media than anywhere else. If you're not a part of a social network, especially Facebook, you are missing an amazing opportunity.

I like what Dan Blank of WeGrowMedia.com says: "Platform is not about status updates, but about being a person others want in their lives."[13] Consider how people who are interested in you and your content may want to connect with you, and grow your platform in that direction.

If you haven't read the previous chapter, take two minutes to review "Step 1: Build Your Platform," which provides recommendations and free resources to check out.

---

9   www.outskirtspress.com/options/16902_3_free_e_book_guides_including_self_publishing_simplified.html.

10   www.createspace.com/pub/services.home.do?tab=PUBLISHING.

11   "Social Networking Reaches Nearly One in Four Around the World," eMarketer, June 18, 2013, www.emarketer.com/Article/Social-Networking-Reaches-Nearly-One-Four-Around-World/1009976.

12   Jay Baer, "11 Shocking New Social Media Statistics in America," www.emarketer.com/Article/Social-Networking-Reaches-Nearly-One-Four-Around-World/1009976.

13   Dan Blank, "Platform is Craft" PDF download available free for signing up to receive his weekly newsletter at www.wegrowmedia.com, p. 6.

Online Platform Resources

If you want some help building or growing certain parts of your online platform (website, blog, branding), check out the resources listed below. For information on marketing and social media, see the Marketing section toward the end of this chapter.

- Dan Peters at www.danpetersdesign.com. He is a great resource for pastors or Christian leaders and churches.
- Toban Penner at www.pennerwebdesign.com. He is a WordPress and SEO (search engine optimization) expert.
- Tyler Goll at www.tylergoll.com. He can perform a number of creative services that will help you build your brand.
- Taylor Carlson at www.gen-comm.com. She does a great job at setting up a simple, attractive blog for you in WordPress or Blogger for an affordable price.
- Andrew Hook at www.thedrewdesign.com. He can get you set up with a good website for an affordable price.
- See Area 4 below for recommended cover designers who also do aspects of design, platform, and brand development.

Area 2: Editing/Proofreading

Finding the right editor for your book is a critical and sometimes challenging process. Letting someone else read your raw manuscript can be a bit like standing naked in the cold—vulnerable and chilling! To find the right editor, look for these qualities:

- Expertise and experience in editing a book. The person needs to have more experience than correcting friends' papers in college. English teachers can give some good feedback about grammar and writing in general (I was an English teacher for eight years). But their input may be limited to what they do in their classroom and may not extend into book writing and the publishing industry. Find someone who has an established, reputable history in the industry, with work you can verify. Some will provide a sample edit upon request.
- Knowledge about writing standards, such as *The Chicago Manual of Style*, which is the style guide resource used by the US book-publishing industry. You'd be surprised how intricate the language can be and how even tiny mistakes throughout your book can undermine your credibility.
- Appreciation for your content, message, and feel over technical accuracy. A sound technician at a concert can do everything technically correct, but if the music doesn't sound good to the audience, people are going to complain. A good editor keeps the message front and center while making its presentation excellent.

- Editing with *your* voice in mind. I've had my share of run-ins with editors who edit books based on how they think something should be said instead of how the author would communicate the content. Review my comments about protecting your voice in chapter 14. Don't be afraid to argue with your editor (with a smile, of course). Professional editors make changes for a reason, so you might learn something. But editors are always learning as well, so share your point of view and determine together how best to communicate your message.

- Ability to provide a quote ahead of time. I recommend not hiring proofreading at an hourly rate. A proofread is straightforward, and a professional should be able to give you a rate based on the number of words or pages. Editing is more intricate and depends of many variables. Ask for a ballpark estimate, but understand it's difficult to determine in advance how much work it will take to fully edit a complete manuscript.

- Willingness to provide regular updates, if the work will take longer than a week to complete, so you can manage the editor's progress.

When it comes time to edit your manuscript, review the content in chapter 14.

Michelle Winger of LiterallyPrecise.com has put together a simple chart showing the difference between proofreading and different levels of editing here.[1] The basic difference is how deep an editor digs into your manuscript. Typically, the more effort an editor puts into your manuscript, the more expensive the fee. A basic proofread is simply checking for technical errors in spelling and punctuation—conforming your manuscript to a writing standard such as *The Chicago Manual of Style*—so that is the cheapest service. Creating content from scratch (like ghostwriting) will be the most expensive. There are many levels of editing in between those two extremes.

Go to these web pages for a more extensive description of the role of a proofreader[2] versus a copyeditor.[3]

Editing/Proofreading Resources

- Elance.com gives you access to a community of more than three million freelancers. Search "editing a book" on their website and you'll find thousands of qualified professionals from around the world to proofread or edit your book.[4] Do your due diligence to find the right one for you.

---

1 www.literallyprecise.com/services/service-levels.

2 www.sfep.org.uk/pub/faqs/fproof.asp.

3 www.sfep.org.uk/pub/faqs/fedit.asp.

4 www.elance.com/category/writing.

- For Christian authors seeking an editor, fill out this <u>form</u>[1] from the <u>Christian Editor Network</u>[2] to find one editor who will suit your needs, or request to be connected with a number of editors who would be good for you. Learn more about their services <u>here</u>.[3] This is a one-stop shop for all your editing needs.
- Kathy Ide is a full-time freelance editor/mentor for new writers, established authors, and book publishers. She has written and ghostwritten books, articles, short stories, devotionals, and curriculum. Her newest book is *Proofreading Secrets of Best-Selling Authors*. Connect with Kathy at <u>www.KathyIde.com</u>.
- Michelle Winger at <u>LiterallyPrecise.com</u> is a grammar enthusiast and a fantastic proofreader for fiction and nonfiction. She provides excellent service with a positive attitude and a quick turnaround.
- Alice Sullivan is a ghostwriter, author, writing coach, speaker, and editor. She has worked on nearly 1,000 books, including eleven *New York Times* best sellers. She works with publishers, agents, and authors to develop books that are both entertaining and memorable. Connect with Alice at <u>www.alicesullivan.com</u>.

Area 3: Interior Design, Layout, and Typesetting

Interior design, layout, formatting, and typesetting all refer to what your content looks like between the front and back cover of your book.

This generally involves someone taking a completed manuscript (usually in Microsoft Word or Apple's Pages) and formatting it into a print-ready PDF that you can send to a printer or upload for print-on-demand.

This process should not start until your manuscript is *completely* done and polished. Adding or removing content can potentially shift the page layout. Don't assume that changing, adding, or removing a few words is a quick, easy fix. Once the content is put into book-layout form, changes will often involve extra fees.

Some books include call-outs or pullouts, which are short quotes that you pull out of your text to emphasize important content on a page. Designers will do this for you as long as you clearly show what sentences you want to highlight.

If you want to try to do this yourself for a lower cost, I recommend purchasing a Word template from <u>www.bookdesigntemplates.com</u>. You'd be surprised how many inconsistencies sneak in when you do it yourself, and these templates will help give your book a more professional look.

1　<u>www.christianeditor.com/authors/authors-seeking-editors.html</u>.

2　<u>www.christianeditor.com</u>.

3　<u>www.christianeditor.com/authors.html</u>.

Hiring someone to lay out/typeset your book can really kick up the quality of your book. I think it's worth the cost, since this is where readers are spending most of their time once they buy the book. Font choice, font size, line spacing, etc., all help to make reading your book a great experience. Below are some resources for professional interior design and typesetting.

Interior Resources

- Katherine Lloyd at TheDESK is an experienced professional who does wonderful work. She can help you with the interior of your book as well as other services you may need, like e-book conversion.[4]

- Some free do-it-yourself Word templates are included here at SelfPublishing.com. They also provide services to have your interior done professionally.[5]

- For specialized interiors, see Tamara Dever at TLC Graphics.[6] They do other high-quality design work as well.

- E-lance.com. Search "typesetting," "book layout," or "book design" and you'll find plenty of freelancers to choose from. Be sure to view their qualifications and portfolios to ensure they have done projects like yours in the past.

- Many online print-on-demand companies have à la carte services that include taking care of the inside of your book. Here are a few I recommend: DogEarPublishing.net, professional services at Lulu.com,[7] Outskirts Press,[8] and CreateSpace.com's professional services.[9]

Area 4: Complete Cover Design

If there were one investment I would encourage you to make, it would be to hire a professional to create your book cover. By *professional* I mean a person who has specific and extensive experience designing book covers for money, not just an artist or someone who has a degree in graphic design.

There are plenty of details in the process from start to end, which include technical considerations so that the final PDF you will upload or send to a printer is all that it needs to be.

---

4   www.thedeskonline.com.

5   www.selfpublishing.com/design/production-center/articles/ms-word/.

6   www.tlcgraphics.com.

7   www.lulu.com/services/.

8   www.outskirtspress.com/options/16902_3_free_e_book_guides_including_self_publishing_simplified. html.

9   www.createspace.com/pub/services.home.do?tab=PUBLISHING.

An awesome cover will not automatically sell your book. But a bad cover will for sure keep it from selling. Designer <u>Yvonne Parks</u> says:

> Cover design is like music. It has a feel and flow that is essential to make an *emotional* connection with a potential reader. The goal of your book's cover is to catch the eye of a potential reader from across a room filled with thousands of books, or if online, among the many book-cover thumbnails on the computer screen. The cover isn't meant to tell the whole story. It's meant to pique the interest of a buyer and hint to the contents of the book. If you can just make them curious, then you're halfway to selling your book simply because you've caused them to pick it up.[1]

I believe a third party should help create your front cover, because this is the one part of your book that will cause a person to either walk past or pick up your book. Typically authors are too closely connected to their content and want to tell the whole story on the cover. Realize that *all* you know is only confusing to those who are just trying to decide whether or not to buy your book.

Potential buyers will look at your front cover for only a few moments. If they're interested, they'll flip the book over (if they have a physical copy) or scroll down to read the book's description (if online). If they are not hooked in 20 seconds, you don't have a sale. It's the winning combination of a curiosity-piquing front cover and intriguing back cover copy that seals the deal and sells your book.

How to Work with a Designer

If you hire a cover designer, talk to her or him about the following:

- The *emotion* you want to evoke with your cover based on the one primary message you want to communicate.
- What primary image or concept will evoke this feeling? Designers appreciate being able to initiate the creative process. However, if you have something firmly in your head about what you want the cover to look like, make those wishes known up front and/or do your own research and find some acceptable images yourself. An Internet search for "stock photos" will provide you with a number of good places to search for the right graphic. Then ask yourself, Is that image unique, or at least not overused? If you've seen the same image before, how can you evoke the same feeling without that overused image?
- Keep the message positive. Even if your nonfiction book addresses a problem, the cover should show that there is a hopeful solution.

---

1   Yvonne Parks designed the cover of this book and is one of the primary cover designers I recommend to others. She is wonderfully talented, very focused and organized, has a track record of winning covers, and is easy to work with. Her website is <u>www.pearcreative.ca</u>.

- Deliver your content *up front*, including all information for the front and back cover I included in Step 5: Design Your Book's Cover in the previous chapter. If the book's genre and target audience (children, teens, young adults, older generation) is not apparent, include it.

Keep in mind, the majority of book buyers are women. They buy books for themselves and for friends, but also for the men in their lives. A book cover doesn't have to be feminine, but it does need to evoke an emotion and make potential readers curious enough to pick it up. All people buy on how something makes them feel. So make them feel something—through the title and subtitle, the primary image, the colors, the fonts, the book description on the back, and even your photo and bio.

What a Designer Will Provide

Most designers will provide the following:

- An initial concept and sometimes up to three mock-ups.
- Two or three rounds of design revisions, which include any last-minute, minor corrections to the text.
- A final, high-resolution, print-ready PDF you can upload to a printer or for print-on-demand.
- A jpeg of your front cover to use for your e-book and promotion on your blog, website, etc. Some designers may provide a 3D image (for free or for a nominal fee) that shows your cover as an actual book.

How to Evaluate Your Cover

Once you have your first round of mock-ups from your designer, review them with these things in mind:

- See with the eyes of your target audience. Just because you like your cover, that doesn't mean they will. Look at the books you've bought in the last three years, or go to your favorite bookstore and see them displayed. Understand your market and create a cover that will appeal to them.
- Be aware of your close, personal connection to your own content. I offend just about every author who brings me a cover concept, even though at the start they tell me they want my honest opinion. Find someone who's willing to tell you your baby is ugly if it is and who will work with you to discover what is best for your book, not just cater to your preferences.
- Find the delicate balance of being true to who you are as the author and making the cover marketable.

Potential readers will assume the quality of your content by the quality of your cover. If you want to communicate that you are a quality writer, invest in a quality cover. People won't spend money on a book that looks bad.

For information on cover options and special treatments like embossing and spot gloss, see Area 5: Printing Your Books below.

Additional Helpful Information

For more details on the process of book cover design:

- Review tips by Michael Hyatt about how to work with a designer, especially his "10 Tips for Developing Eye-Popping Packaging."[1]
- Along with my "What to Avoid" section in the previous chapter, also see Joel Friedlander's "Self-Publishing Authors: Don't Fall Into These Cover Design Traps!"[2]
- See the article "Your Book Cover is Like a Highway Billboard" by Scott Lorenz.[3]
- Read Melody Simmons's helpful article about using stock images legally, "All About Stock Images and Book Covers."[4] Melody also provides a list of sites where you can purchase stock images.

How I Created My Cover

Because cover design is so important, here is an insider's look at the process I take authors through and some of the issues to consider for your book. To help you ponder the issues you need to consider, I'm going to review the process I went through personally to create the cover for this book.

The graphic below shows the six covers that Yvonne Parks designed for me. You'll notice that the title in these mocks is *Anyone Can Write*. I printed one small run of books for two workshops before changing the title. I explain the reason behind the change below.

If you look closely, you'll notice that there are a few variations on the subtitle. That's because I was trying out some ideas.

I walked into the process considering the following:

- **My audience.** Although many people want to write a book, I was seeking to appeal mostly to mature, experienced leaders—male and female. The cover had to appeal

---

1   www.michaelhyatt.com/10-tips-for-developing-eye-popping-packaging.html.

2   www.createspace.com/en/community/docs/DOC-1511.

3   www.writersfunzone.com/blog/2013/08/07/your-book-cover-is-like-a-highway-billboard-by-scott-lorenz/.

4   www.ebookindiecovers.com/2013/03/31/all-about-stock-images-and-book-covers/.

to men, even though women buy far more books than men. I was okay with
having it appeal to men more than women, but it couldn't alienate either audience.

- **The feel**. The emotions I wanted the cover to evoke included professionalism, excellence, creativity, and empowerment to write and publish a book.

- **The message**. The message of the book that had to come through is "You can write a book, and I'll make it as easy as possible for you to get your book done."

- **My personal taste**. I wanted the cover to feel good to me personally. It's my book. It represents me and I had to like it.

- **Marketability**. The cover had to clearly stand out in a thumbnail image since my "store" is Amazon.com. The design also had to look great for both paperback and e-book formats.

As you know, the winner was sample 2. I'll look at each of the designs briefly and explain the thought process behind each one.

sample 1

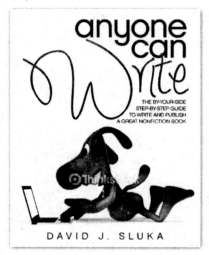

sample 2

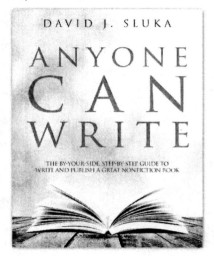

sample 2B

sample 3

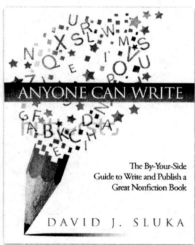

sample 4

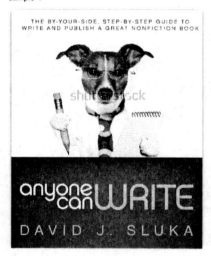

sample 5

pearcreative.ca

Sample 4: I'm starting with Sample 4 because this was my initial concept. The title of my book was inspired by Chef Gusteau's book *Anyone Can Cook* in the movie *Ratatouille*. Since a writing rat wasn't going to work, I sent Yvonne a link to <u>one</u>,[1] <u>two</u>,[2] <u>three</u>[3] cavemen, but she didn't feel that would

1   www.contentwritingusa.com/wp-content/uploads/2011/01/Chiseling-Caveman-e1295104424454.jpg.

2   http://1.bp.blogspot.com/_GCOdfw1WiCg/S-3VUSBUu_I/AAAAAAAAAAM/Zt2lxaRaLcw/s1600-R/caveman.gif.

3   http://i.istockimg.com/file_thumbview_approve/9726295/2/stock-illustration-9726295-caveman-using-a-computer.jpg.

appeal to women. And she didn't think anyone wanted to be compared to a monosyllabic, grunting, hairy dumb guy.

Okay…so I work with people on their book covers all the time and *my* first idea was a bad one. At least I got the ball rolling and checked off something that wouldn't work.

Then I found the dog image in Sample 4. (You'll notice that there is a watermark for Shutterstock across the image. That's not the dog's mustache. It's there because anyone can download the image and see what it looks like for free, but to make the watermark disappear you have to purchase the image.) Personally I like Sample 4 better than the cover that won, and some friends I polled liked it too. But the cover wasn't going to accomplish my most important goals, so it didn't win. Sigh.

Sample 1: Since we were on the dog theme, Yvonne saw this image and threw it in as an option.

Sample 2B: Yvonne liked the font treatment in Sample 1's design, so she created 2B with Sample 2's graphic but with Sample 1's font treatment.

Sample 5: When Yvonne pitched this one to me, I loved the simplicity of it. But for some reason I didn't like the short, computer-generated-looking pencil. As I look at it now, I like it more. I liked the font treatment a lot, and this design got several votes from people I polled.

Sample 4: This was the second concept that came to mind after the dog. I love the red (it's my company brand's theme color) and the exploding pencil—as if creativity is coming out as you write, or all of the many things you could say are being channeled into one clear message through the pencil. But I received feedback that the image was too cluttered and created feelings of confusion.

If I had chosen this cover, I would have made the red bar across the middle that contains the title a little thicker. There is a lot going on behind the title, and it would be very hard to see the title immediately and clearly in a thumbnail image. I still really like this cover, but my feedback said it wasn't going to evoke the feelings I was shooting for.

Sample 2: This design received by far the most and best feedback from the male and female leaders I polled (the audience I work with most and the primary audience I'm trying to appeal to). That is one of the main reasons I didn't go with Sample 4. Sample 4's image emphasized that *anyone* can write, even a dog, but my primary audience wasn't just "anyone." I was shooting for people who have expertise and experience.

The title of Sample 2 emphasizes that anyone *can* write, which is the message I'm trying to send. Samples 1, 2B, and 4 emphasize that anyone can *write*. Samples 3 and 5 weigh all the words equally.

(As you know I changed the title to *Write Your Book*. I decided to make the change for three reasons:

1. For consistent branding since this is the name of my workshop and domain (www. write-your-book.com).
2. Some professional writers don't believe that just "anyone can write" and the idea would hinder them from recommending my book to others. Plus I know people who can't write and hire me to write for them. It's like when a couple says, "We're

going to build our own home." I know a couple who did that on their own, but what is meant most of the time is that the couple will make the major decisions and pick out everything that goes into the house, but some builders will be the ones doing the actual work.

3. As non-sexy and non-creative as the title is, I wanted the title to be clear and directive. I want you to "write your book.") Okay, back to cover design.

Sample 2 has a classic, timeless font that will not be going out of style next year.

I also wanted to show the end product of an author's hard work—a completed book—versus the instrument to complete the product—a pencil or computer. The combination of the image and the font treatment for the title seemed to evoke the emotion I was shooting for.

After sorting through the feedback I received, it would have been unwise to go with any other cover. I ended up darkening the title font and making the subtitle bigger, but Sample 2 is what ended up as the cover design for this book.

I tell you all this to demonstrate how you can think through your cover. Combine this process with insights you receive from the "How to Work with a Designer" section above.

Evaluating Feedback

Getting feedback on your cover can be a good thing and a bad thing, depending on whom you ask and how you process the feedback. My advice is to get feedback, but take these recommendations into consideration:

- **Be strategic about who you ask**. Send your cover out to a small "focus group" of trusted friends or people you know who will give you honest feedback. Make sure that most of the people in that group represent the primary audience you want to reach. Otherwise you'll just have a bunch of opinions that don't really count toward book sales.

  I posted the six cover graphics above on my Facebook page for feedback. Yvonne posted them on hers as well. Our goal was to see who would respond and what my primary audience had to say. I also sent out a private e-mail to about 10 leaders/authors I've worked with, asking for their feedback. I'm not sure I'd recommend for everyone to put his or her cover mock-ups on Facebook. I did because I knew what I was looking for and how to filter the feedback.

- **Ask specific questions** from your reviewers, like "*What does the cover say to you? What do you feel when you see the cover? When you read the title and subtitle, what do you think you're going to get out of reading the book? Is anything on the cover getting in the way of your buying the book?*"

- **Filter the feedback wisely**. I have some pretty awesome Facebook designer-type friends and professionals who provided some great input. But some came at design differently, so they made recommendations that I had to process and in the end did not implement. As you filter through feedback, consider who said it (if they represent your primary audience), what they are really trying to say, why they are saying it, and how much weight you should apply to their opinions. The best thing about feedback is that it gets you going somewhere. Make sure your "somewhere" is a better place and not into a state of depression and confusion. Feedback can be overwhelming. So go at it with a stable, steady heart.

- **Remember that your cover is not about you**…mostly. You need to feel good about your cover, but I've run into many situations where the author loves the cover but it would only sell to his or her mother and a few loyal followers. Try to see your cover from your primary audience's point of view.

- **Keep your goal the priority**. The goal of your cover is to sell your book. Period. If you're going to give your book away for free, make it attractive enough for someone to want to open and read it. If you're writing only for posterity, make the cover attractive enough so when your great-great-grandkids find your book eighty years from now, they will at least think you're cool with good taste in design.

Cover Design Resources

The following are cover designers I have worked with successfully in the past. A designer who is both excellent and trustworthy is a priceless find. I put each of these people in that category. Prices will vary by designer and the work you want them to do. If you check out their websites, you'll find that they do much more than just cover design.

- Yvonne Parks at www.pearcreative.ca
- Steve Fryer at www.stevefryer.com
- Ken Vail at www.prevailcreative.com
- Carl Butel at www.deepimage.net.au
- Tamara Dever at www.tlcgraphics.com

www.99designs.com is another resource I recommend. You can create a design brief describing your project, choose a design package based on your budget, launch the contest, receive dozens of designs to consider from their community of more than 250,000 designers around the world, provide feedback on the designs you like, and then choose a winner. The contest process takes seven days. I've known people who have had good success with 99designs.com, and I've viewed some excellent covers from the designers on this site.

This is a great option if you're on a limited budget and want many options to choose from. Your budget will determine the number and quality of options submitted by freelancers for you to review.

Because I work with many authors on their books, my approach has been to work with a few professionals I can trust and build relationships with them long term. I can't afford to roll the dice each time I have to help an author with a book. But if you're doing it on your own, 99designs.com may be a great option for you.

crowdSPRING provides similar services with a similar setup as 99designs.com. They also provide other design services.[1]

Search "indie cover design" on the Internet and a world of opportunities will present itself.

Area 5: Printing Your Books

Today's print-on-demand services allow you to print only as many copies of your book as you need (even if it's only one). Due to limited printing options in the past, too many authors purchased hundreds or thousands of books and still have boxes of them in storage. Don't be that person.

Printing a larger quantity at one time will give you a better price per book, but printing on demand—printing as books are needed—is usually a better option. Unless you have a place to store the books and can guarantee they will sell in three to six months, I think smaller print runs (under 500 copies) is the way to go.

With e-books on the rise, some people think that printed books will soon be obsolete. For one point of view on the importance of printing your book, see this article by Bowker.[2] Another helpful article about print on demand service pros and cons is on WriterBeware.com.[3] There are still people who like to hold books in their hands, so making your book available in paperback is still a good idea.

There are advantages of printing in larger quantities on an offset press. The most obvious is a lower price per book, which means greater profits for you. Another benefit is that offset lithographic printing offers you cover treatment options that are not available digitally. (See the Special Cover Treatments section below.)

Most offset printers have a minimum quantity of 1,000 (or sometimes 500) per print run. If you need fewer than 500 copies of your book), you will have to print digitally. Digital printing is fast, and the quality has become quite excellent. To the untrained eye it's hard to see the difference between digital and offset lithographic printing.

---

1   www.crowdspring.com/how-it-works/.

2   www.selfpublishedauthor.com/content/opportunity-knocking-why-authors-should-go-print.

3   www.sfwa.org/other-resources/for-authors/writer-beware/pod/.

Short-Run Digital Printing Resources

If you publish with CreateSpace.com, print-on-demand is a part of their services. No matter how many you print, the cost is the same.

If you're looking for more than 50 books, with lower prices for greater quantities, here are some great resources:

- Snowfall Press. See their cost calculator.[4] Their website has a list of professionals for various areas on their expert community page. This is a great printer that also supports international printing needs.

- 48 Hour Books prints books within 48 hours of the time you upload your files.[5] They can do same-day print and ship as well. See their cost calculator for an immediate quote on printing and shipping your book.[6] I have worked with 48 Hour Books a number of times, always with a very good outcome. Their customer service is excellent and the quality of books very good.

- InstantPublisher.com is a full-service printing company that does all of their work in-house. They have a helpful and immediate price quote calculator here.[7] Their minimum quantity is 25 books. Great customer service.

- BooksJustBooks.com is one of the Internet's first commercial printing services. They have a network of printers around the United States for both digital and offset printing.

- Lightning-Press.com provides affordable hardcover and softcover short-run digital printing (25–2,000 is their specialty).

- All of the large-run printing companies listed in the following section can also provide short-run printing at pricing comparable to (sometimes better than) those listed above. But they will not print ones and twos; 50 or 100 is usually a minimum quantity for their digital presses.

- Search "digital printing" and the name of your city on the Internet and you may find a printer in your area so you can avoid shipping costs.

Whichever printer you choose, it's always a good idea to view a hard proof before printing a number of books.

---

4   http://app.snowfallpress.com/SpineCalc.html.

5   www.48hrbooks.com.

6   www.48hrbooks.com/Self-Publishing-Cost.

7   www.instantpublisher.com/Price-quote.aspx.

Large-Run Printing Resources

The following resources provide smaller runs for digital printing, and also larger runs on their offset presses. A minimum (usually 500 or 1,000) is required for higher-quality offset printing and additional cover treatment options.

- BethanyPress.com prints only Christian books. Minimum for offset printing is 1,000 copies.

- BangPrinting.com. Minimum for offset is 500 copies. Bang Printing offers other services like order fulfillment.

- Bookmasters.com. One thousand copies is most economical for their offset printing. Bookmasters also provides other services such as distribution, fulfillment, editorial, and marketing.

- BooksJustBooks.com has a network of printers around the United States for both digital and offset printing.

Special Cover Treatments

Most digital printers offer only one type of paperback cover: gloss. CreateSpace.com has recently started to offer matte as well as gloss.

When you print a larger number of books using an offset press, not only does your cost go down considerably, but you also have additional cover options available. Printers call these options by different names, but here is a description of four basic options to consider besides gloss or matte:

- **Matte and gloss mix** (Bethany Press calls this MatteKote, or "coating" the cover with a matte finish). For this durable finish, the printer first lays down a gloss coat over the cover. Then the cover passes through the press a second time, coating it with a matte finish. You can leave the cover all matte, or you can choose to cover only certain parts of the cover with matte so that the gloss underneath shines through. This creates a shine or glimmer on the parts that remain gloss. You can have as little or as much shine as you want for the same cost. This treatment is often only a few cents more per book, and it creates a nice effect for your cover.

- **Spot gloss** (also called Spot UV, UV coating, or UV varnish). This treatment puts gloss on specific spots on top of the existing cover finish. It makes what you choose to gloss stand out more than if it was behind the matte like in the previous option.

- **Emboss**. You can emboss or raise a graphic or certain lettering on your cover. You can combine embossing with the above treatments so that your embossed portions shine and other parts of the cover are flat or matte, making the effect even more noticeable.

- **Hard cover**. You can print the design directly on the hard cover, or you can print on a jacket to go around the cover. The features above are available on a hard cover and its jacket as well.

I recommend talking to the printer about what options might look good with your specific cover design. They are the experts and can tell you what's going to look the best.

Your cover designer will need to know how to create proper print files for these special treatments. The printer can provide feedback to make sure the files accurately represent what you want to do.

Whenever you do a specialty cover, be sure you have crystal-clear communication with the printer. Don't assume anything. See a proof if you can, or have your representative tell you specifically what you'll receive. It's no fun paying extra for a special feature and then getting something different from what you were thinking.

Area 6: E-Books

The *e* in "e-book" stands for *electronic*. So an e-book is an electronic copy of the cover and text of your book that can be read on an e-reader like a Kindle or NOOK, or by an app on a tablet or computer.

To publish an e-book, the cover and inside text must be converted to e-book format. The most popular digital format is e-pub, which is supported by the largest number of e-readers, including the NOOK and the iPad. Kindle does not support e-pub; it has its own proprietary format. PDFs of books are sometimes considered e-books because a PDF is an electronic file.

Forty-three percent of Americans ages sixteen and older own a tablet or an e-book reader.[1] E-book sales have grown dramatically over the last few years (more than 4,400 percent since 2008),[2] and e-books are here to stay. If you are going to publish a book in print, publish an e-book version too.

Some authors choose to publish only an e-book. Three benefits of this include:

- **Fast to market**. Within twenty-four hours after uploading your final files (sometimes longer depending on the service you use), your e-book is available for purchase.
- **Less expensive**. For e-books, you only create a front-cover image, saving on full-cover costs. For the interior, you can do it yourself or pay someone a minimal fee to convert your manuscript to e-book format.

---

1   Lee Rainie and Aaron Smith, "Tablet and E-Reader Ownership Update," Pew Internet & American Life Project, October 18, 2013, www.pewinternet.org/Reports/2013/Tablets-and-ereaders.aspx, accessed January 2, 2014.

2   "E-book sales are up 43%, but that's still a 'slowdown,'" USA Today, May 16, 2013, www.usatoday.com/story/life/books/2013/05/15/e-book-sales/2159117/.

- **Ongoing changes.** This is especially helpful for nonfiction books that contain data or information that becomes outdated quickly. You make the changes and the updated e-book is available within twenty-four hours (sometimes longer depending on the service you use).

Take a few minutes to read a helpful overview at CNET Reviews on "How to self-publish an e-book."[1]

If you haven't read chapter 16 of this book, I recommend reading Step 7: Convert Your File to E-Book Format and Make Available Online. You'll find more in-depth information about Amazon. com's Kindle Direct Publishing and Smashwords.

E-Book Resources

All of the companies below can convert your manuscript to the necessary format and distribute it to e-book retailers. There are many other ways to get your book converted to e-book format and available for download at popular online stores, but these are the resources I've used the most or can recommend.

- If you're thinking about purchasing a book design template from BookDesignTemplates.com, consider buying one of their 2Way Templates,[2] which combines the best features of their print and e-book templates together into one streamlined file that can be used for both formats. This helps you avoid an extra e-book conversion fee.
- www.BookBaby.com provides everything you need to publish professionally and distribute your book on Amazon, Apple, Kobo, Barnes & Noble, Sony, and many other popular retailers in more than 170 countries around the globe. I've worked with BookBaby and have always been very happy with their work and customer service. They can also print hard copies of your book.[3]
- Kindle Direct Publishing.[4] See chapter 16 for an extensive review of KDP.
- Smashwords is the largest distributor of independently published (indie) e-books.[5] It's fast and free for any author or publisher, anywhere in the world, to publish and distribute e-books to major retailers. Smashwords's founder, Mark Coker, maintains Mark's List, which is a list of low-cost e-book formatters and cover

1   http://reviews.cnet.com/8301-18438_7-20010547-82/how-to-self-publish-an-ebook/.
2   www.bookdesigntemplates.com/template-gallery/#2Way
3   http://print.bookbaby.com.
4   http://kdp.amazon.com.
5   www.smashwords.com.

designers with prices starting at about $50. You can get the list via instant auto-responder by e-mailing list@smashwords.com or go <u>here</u>.[6]

- If you prefer Barnes & Noble over Amazon.com, check out <u>www.nookpress.com</u>. They are very comparable to KDP.

Area 7: Audio Book

You've already done the hard part of writing your book. Through Amazon's <u>Audiobook Creation Exchange</u> (ACX), you can make it available for people to purchase from Amazon.com, audible.com, or iTunes. You can narrate the book yourself or use the site to find someone to do it for you.

Area 8: ISBNs and Bar Codes

ISBNs and bar codes seem to cause the most confusion with authors. For an overview about what ISBNs are all about for self-publishers, see <u>ISBN 101 for Self-Publishers</u> by Joel Friedlander.[7] A very helpful article.

Here are the basics of what you need to know.

ISBN means "International Standard Book Number." It is a unique number that identifies your book in a worldwide numbering system. Not every book requires an ISBN. You can print and sell your book without an ISBN, but an ISBN is required if you want to sell your book commercially in a retail channel (like at a bookstore or online). It's the way stores identify your book, in each format of your book (one for the paperback, another for the e-book).

A bar code is a representation of your ISBN via a series of vertical bars. A bar code for a book looks like this:

It's placed in the bottom-right corner on the back cover of a book so that a product scanner can quickly read the ISBN, price, and other bibliographic information attached to your ISBN.

You only need a bar code if you're going to sell your book in bookstores, but I recommend having one regardless of where or how you sell your books.

---

6   www.smashwords.com/list.

7   www.thebookdesigner.com/2010/11/isbn-101-for-self-publishers/.

Subsidy publishers or companies like CreateSpace create a barcode for you and put it on the cover. You can create your own bar code free here,[1] or you can pay a small fee to www.createbarcodes. com, Bowker, or another authorized ISBN agency.

How to Obtain an ISBN

There are four basic ways to obtain an ISBN:

1. Purchase one or more from Bowker Identifier Services and become your own publisher.[2] To truly publish your book yourself, you must create your own account with Bowker (or your country's agency), or an authorized agent, then purchase one or more ISBNs. (See the section on Buying Your Own ISBNs below for more information on this.) Certain companies can also help you be your own publisher like Self-Publishing.com, BelieversPress.com, and MorganJamesPublishing.com.

2. Publish with a subsidy publisher (like Xulon Press), and they will provide an ISBN as part of the package. They will be listed as your publisher and will have certain rights to your book and its files. It's very important to know what those rights are before you sign a contract.

3. Publish with CreateSpace.com, DogEarPublishing.net, Lulu.com, BookBaby.com, Kindle Direct Publishing,[3] or another self-publishing service for print or e-book, and they will provide an ISBN for you for free or for a small fee. They will be listed as your publisher since you are using their platform to distribute your book, but you retain all rights to your book and its files.

4. Publish as an independent publisher. CreateSpace.com offers a Custom ISBN and Custom Universal ISBN, which allows you to have your own unique imprint name and not have them listed as your publisher.[4] Publisher Services, the largest authorized agent of the US ISBN Agency, has an Independent Publisher Program and a Personalized Publisher Program.[5] There are other authorized agents that offer different deals, such as www.isbnservices.com.

    These are great if you're going to publish just one title. For more than one ISBN, I feel it's best to choose option 1 above.

---

1   www.tux.org/~milgram/bookland/.

2   www.myidentifiers.com.

3   http://kdp.amazon.com.

4   www.createspace.com/Products/Book/ISBNs.jsp.

5   www.isbn-us.com.

Resources for Buying Your Own ISBNs

Bowker Identifier Services is the official registration agency of ISBNs in the US or any of its territories. For other countries, go here to find your official agency.[6]

As of January 2014, pricing for ISBNs with Bowker is:

- $125 for one.

- $250 for ten. This is the best option for most people. If you are going to have a paperback and an e-book, you'll need two ISBNs, which is the same price as buying ten.

- $575 for one hundred. $1,000 for one thousand. They have bulk pricing for more than a thousand.

By purchasing your own block of ISBNs from Bowker, you are creating your own publishing company or imprint. You don't have to file documents with the government, as you would to form a business. You only need to name your imprint and provide contact information for your group of ISBNs. It's as simple as that.

As you use each ISBN, you fill in bibliographical information for that title, which then registers your book with the Books in Print database (www.BooksInPrint.com), providing worldwide availability. If you're curious to know what it takes to register a title, this is a step-by-step PDF explaining the simple process.[7]

Bowker also offers its own self-publishing services, which provides some options that other companies do not, like a book-sales widget and viewing the book as an Android app.[8]

My Recommendation for ISBNs

If you are on a tight budget and are only going to publish one book, publish with a company like CreateSpace.com. You have complete control and rights to the content. CreateSpace will be identified as your publisher in the bibliographic database.

There are some limitations if a subsidy press uses their ISBN for your book. Research what your rights are (and are not) so you're not disappointed down the road.

If you plan to self-publish more than one book, create your own publishing company and buy a block of ten ISBNs.

---

6   www.isbn-international.org/agency.

7   www.myidentifiers.com/sites/default/files/images/Title_setup_and_registration.pdf.

8   www.myidentifiers.com/self_publisher.

Area 9: Fulfillment and Distribution

Fulfillment is when a company warehouses a large quantity of your books and *fulfills* an order for your book after someone buys it. Fulfillment allows you to print a larger number of books (lowering the cost per book), store them, and then ship them out as needed.

Distribution usually means the way the books get from the publisher or printer to the bookstore where customers can buy your book. Baker & Taylor and Ingram are considered the biggest distributors/wholesalers. Other distributors usually sell to them, and they in turn sell to the retailers.

MillCityPress has a good summary of fulfillment and distribution here.[1]

I've given a very simplistic explanation of this process since most readers of this book will not require or use these services. You can get basically the same services for free by fulfilling your book orders through CreateSpace's print-on-demand and getting your book distributed to online retailers, bookstores, libraries, and academic institutions through their Extended Distribution Program.[2] See this article for additional reasons to go with CreateSpace versus a distributor for self-publishing.[3]

Fulfillment and Distribution Resources

If you are looking for fulfillment and distribution resources, here are my recommendations.

- MillCityPress.net offers website order fulfillment, print-on-demand and expanded distribution.[4]
- Bookmasters.com offers fulfillment and distribution.[5]
- BethanyPress.com and BelieversPress.com offer global distribution through their partnership with Anchor Distributors or see www.anchordistribution.com.[6]
- BangPrinting.com offers inventory fulfillment.[7]
- MicahTek offers warehousing,[8] order fulfillment,[9] and other services.

---

1   www.millcitypress.net/wholesale-vs-retail-distribution.

2   www.createspace.com/Products/Book/ExpandedDistribution.jsp.

3   www.selfpubbootcamp.com/2012/08/11/book-distribution-a-qa/.

4   www.millcitypress.net/publishing/services/website-order-fulfillment and www.millcitypress.net/types-of-book-distribution.

5   www.bookmasters.com/services/fulfillment/ and http://www.bookmasters.com/services/distribution/.

6   www.bethanypress.com/distribute/global-distribution/ and www.believerspress.com/distribute/global-distribution/.

7   www.bangprinting.com/promail/fulfillment.htm.

8   www.micahtek.com/warehousing.shtml.

9   www.micahtek.com/product_fulfillment.shtml.

- See <u>fulfillment</u> by Amazon.[10]

My Recommendation for Fulfillment and Distribution

For most people looking to self-publish, it makes a lot of sense (and cents) to use a print-on-demand fulfillment and distribution service like CreateSpace.com for selling ones and twos from your website and other online stores like Amazon.com. Do you really want to pay for fulfillment and distribution or do it yourself by having a load of books in storage, and when you receive each order, package up the book, go to the post office, mail the package, track the package, and take customer calls if there's a problem?

If you are in front of large audiences and have the opportunity to go through hundreds of books over a few months, and if you have a place to store ten or more boxes of books, you can print a large number of books at one time and pay a lower per-book cost. By printing 500–1,000 or more at one time using an offset press, you can raise the quality of your book a bit more and include a special cover treatment (see Area 5 above).

In summary, for sales from your website and online, and for smaller print runs as needed, do print-on-demand. If you speak at large gatherings or if you're selling a large number of books throughout the year, *also* print a larger run of books at a printer.

Area 10: Marketing and Networking

Marketing is how you let others know about your book and help them see it as a resource they want to buy.

Here are some creative and inexpensive ways to market your book:

- **Create a package**. If you're a leader or speaker, you probably have other resources available to you that you can bundle with your book: a PowerPoint presentation, an MP3 of a recent talk that is related to your book's topic, a study guide, a transcription of a short talk, 30 minutes of free consultation (be sure you can do what you promise), your "Top Ten Tips for Whatever" formatted into a nice-looking resource. Be creative and think of something you already have that you could bundle with your book. If you don't have anything, put something together quickly and inexpensively.

- **Do a book launch**. Dan Blank at <u>www.WeGrowMedia.com</u> has a great <u>article</u> about how to plan a book launch.[11]

---

10 <u>http://services.amazon.com/fulfillment-by-amazon/benefits.htm</u>.

11 <u>www.wegrowmedia.com/the-anxiety-and-enthusiasm-of-launching-a-book/</u>.

- **Book-signing party**. When your book becomes available, invite friends and others who may be interested to a book-release party. It'll probably cost you something to do this—at a minimum refreshments, unless you can talk your friends into pitching in. Make it doable for you and celebrate.

- **Run special promotions**. Within CreateSpace and Kindle Direct Publishing there are ways to run special deals. Check out those resources for more information, then expand them with ideas of your own.

- **Continue to build your platform**. A short, thin diving board doesn't have much stability or spring. It's the same way with what you have to stand on as you launch your book. Go deeper, longer, and wider in the way you build your platform—not just for this book, but for you as a person to share what you have.

- **Provide excerpts from your book** on your blog, website, or other social media venues. CreateSpace and KDP provide the "Look Inside" feature for their books so potential buyers can get a taste of what they're buying. Since you own the content and the right to copy, you could provide a free PDF download of the first chapter or selected excerpts on your website. Reprint excerpts strategically in other places: your blog, a magazine, newspaper article, other people's websites. I've repurposed certain parts of this book for my blog—keeping the length under 500 words and choosing parts that would spark interest to potential buyers. Reach out to sources who may be interested in your content and pitch it to them. They'll usually be looking for something that matches their usual publication word count (online articles are often 500 to 900 words), so be ready to tweak and customize your content if asked.

- **Guest host**. Writing for other people's blogs or websites is a great way to do something for someone else and give some exposure to you as a person and your book(s). Peter Sandeen has a great list of guest-blogging sites,[1] or inquire at websites, blogs, magazines, or news sources that may benefit from your content. Freely give and you will freely receive.

Marketing Resources

Some of the companies I've already mentioned also have marketing services.

---

1 www.petersandeen.com/list-of-guest-blogging-sites.

- Online marketing, social media marketing, and traditional book publicity are available <u>here</u> at MillCityPress.[2]

- Bookmasters has <u>publicity and marketing services</u>.[3]

- PR and marketing at <u>TLC Graphics and Narrow Gate Books</u>.[4]

- <u>Marketing tools</u> by BelieversPress.com.[5]

- <u>This link</u> on Dan Poynter's ParaPublishing.com has great information about marketing, promoting, and distributing your book.[6]

- Read a good <u>overview about book marketing</u> for self-publishers by JC Publishing.[7]

I subscribe to a number of blogs that teach me a lot about marketing. Below are those I presently follow. Find a few that interest you. When you sign up, they usually provide a free download of some kind.

- <u>Seth Godin</u>.[8] Author, blogger, speaker, and marketer.
- <u>Jeff Walker.com</u>, creator of the Product Launch Formula.
- Bernadette Jiwa and her company, <u>The Story of Telling</u>.[9]
- Danny Iny and <u>Firepole Marketing</u>.[10]
- <u>Amy Porterfield</u>[11]—social media expert, including <u>Facebook Marketing</u>.[12]
- Sandy Krakowski at <u>www.arealchange.com</u>. Forbes puts Sandy among the top 50 social media power influencers and the top 20 female social media influencers in the world. Her <u>blog</u>[13] offers a ton of free marketing advice.

---

2   <u>www.millcitypress.net/book-marketing-services</u>.

3   <u>www.bookmasters.com/services/marketing/</u>.

4   <u>www.tlcgraphics.com/tlc-wp/services-marketing/</u>.

5   <u>www.believerspress.com/distribute/marketing-publicity/</u>.

6   <u>www.parapublishing.com/sites/para/information/promote.cfm</u>.

7   <u>www.jcpublishers.net/page.php?17</u>.

8   <u>www.sethgodin.typepad.com</u>.

9   <u>www.thestoryoftelling.com</u>.

10   <u>www.firepolemarketing.com</u>.

11   <u>www.amyporterfield.com</u>.

12   <u>www.fbinfluence.com</u>.

13   <u>www.arealchange.com/blog</u>.

- Allen D'Angelo's <u>BookMarketingBlast.com</u>[1] and Publisher's Marketing Action Toolkit at <u>BookCovers.com</u>.[2]

- <u>Publishing Poynters</u>. A monthly newsletter containing book and information-marketing news and ideas from Dan Poynter.[3]

- Nina Amir at <u>www.writenonfictionnow.com</u>.

- <u>Peter Sandeen</u>.[4] Conversion optimization expert and marketing strategist.

- <u>D Bnonn Tennant</u>.[5] Copywriter, web designer, and conversion-rate optimization coach. Offers honest, straightforward, no-punches-pulled marketing advice.

- <u>RayEdwards.com</u>. Direct-response copywriter, marketing strategist, author, and speaker.

- <u>MichaelHyatt.com</u>. Focuses on leadership, productivity, publishing, building a platform, and personal development.

- <u>AdrianneMunkacsy.com</u>. Adrianne is a copywriter with a gift for writing copy in your voice, which can include text for your website, sales page, launch e-mails, newsletters, About page/bio, profile, taglines, or whatever you need.[6]

- Dan Blank at <u>www.wegrowmedia.com</u> helps writers share their stories and connect with readers.

- Steve Spillman's weekly Author Tips and marketing services at <u>www.truepotentialmedia.com</u>.

Networking

Networking is related to marketing because it's how you connect with others so they get to know you, your expertise and experience, and how you share what you have with others.

Networking is a fantastic way to open doors for you and your book. And you'd be surprised how many doors can open once one does. Consider one or more of the following:

---

1   <u>www.bookmarketingblast.com</u>.

2   <u>www.bookcovers.com</u>.

3   <u>www.parapub.com</u>

4   <u>www.petersandeen.com</u>.

5   <u>www.informationhighwayman.com</u>.

6   <u>www.adriannemunkacsy.com</u>.

- Attend a writers' conference. Search "writers conference" on the Internet for one that works for you. Two popular and reputable conferences are Writer's Digest Conference[7] and Author101 University.[8]

- Interact with other authors and industry professionals while taking online writing classes. Check out San Francisco Writers University for free and paid subscription classes.

- Reach out to others in your network. Let them know you're writing a book. You may find you have some knowledgeable friends you didn't know about.

- Join a writers' club. There are probably local chapters near where you live. If you are a Christian author, check out Christian Writers Guild led by *New York Times* best-selling author Jerry B. Jenkins.[9] They have some great conferences, courses, contests, and other helpful writing resources.

- Find authors who live in your area. Take them out for coffee or lunch and ask them to tell their story. Listen and take notes.

- Start following other's blogs and join the conversation by adding helpful comments. The goal is not to promote or sell your book, but rather build relationships and do something for *that* blog. The good you do there will come back around in due time. If you're looking for some good blogs, start with this list of "100 Blogs You Need in Your Life" from LeavingWorkBehind.com.

- Write for another blog. Peter Sandeen has a great list of guest-blogging sites.[10] Or inquire at websites, blogs, magazines, or news sources that may benefit from your content.

Your Assignment

- Consider what kind of a platform you want. Do something to create a way for your audience to interact with you and so you can build relationships with them.

---

7   www.writersdigestconference.com.

8   www.author101university.com.

9   www.christianwritersguild.com.

10   www.petersandeen.com/list-of-guest-blogging-sites.

- Decide *where* you want help, and in what package you want that help to come. Some companies provide a package. Or you can do the work you want to do yourself. Do what you do best and find some reliable professionals to do the rest.

CHAPTER 18

Whatever You Do, Write Your Book

*If you have something to say, then prepare it, write it, and share it
with the audience you have right now. Who knows? Another book
might be waiting just around the corner.*

If you're reading this chapter, hopefully your manuscript is complete and almost ready to upload to print. The world is full of good ideas that have stayed inside people. So if your manuscript isn't done yet, do what it takes to get your book written and published for others to read.

Please contact me if there's anything I can do to encourage or help you further so you can complete your book. For ongoing encouragement and growth as an author, you can sign up to receive my weekly blog at www.david-sluka.com.

I blog at least once a week on Tuesdays on three main topics: communication, publishing, and leadership. About twice a month I also share inspirational content from an author I have worked with in the past or am working with presently, or provide an interview giving a behind-the-scenes look at his or her life as a communicator and leader.

The "How I Write" section shares insights on how different authors approach writing.[1] From time to time I or the authors I work with give me free books to give away to my subscribers. To make sure you don't miss my newest posts and great resources for leaders and communicators, you can subscribe and receive all my posts via e-mail.[2]

Words Can Change the World

Your words are important. Words change minds, which change future actions. Your words can change the world.

I leave you with a quote from Seth Godin that encourages writers to find what works for them and then do it:

---

1   See the tabs for Communication, Publishing, Leadership, Inspiration, and How I Write at www.david-sluka.com.

2   www.david-sluka.com/get-updates.

The process advice that makes sense to me is to write. Constantly. At length. Often. Don't publish everything you write, but the more you write, the more you have to choose from.[1]

My best advice to anyone seeking to write a great book—and I trust you are one of those people—is to:

Prepare your book.

Write your book.

Share your book.

Celebrate!

Write your next book!

---

1   Seth Godin, "Q&A: The writing process," Seth Godin blog posted July 22, 2013, www.sethgodin.typepad. com/seths_blog/2013/07/qa.html.

APPENDIX A

I Just Want to Get Started

If you just want to start writing your book, here's a quick to-do list for you. If needed, consult specific chapters in this book that go into each of these areas in more detail with additional helpful tips. Write inspired and have fun!

Scenario 1: You're Starting Your Book

A general list of things to do includes the following:

1. Create a detailed outline for your book. If you want to know what to include in your outline, see chapters 7 through 10. In general, the goal is to be able, at a glance, to see where you are going and be satisfied with your destination.

2. Ensure that your outline aligns with your purpose, message, and audience (see chapter 11).

3. Set up your document to avoid having to undo a bunch of things later (see chapter 12).

4. Write your book following your outline (see chapter 13).

5. As you are writing, build your platform to promote your book (purchase and read Michael Hyatt's book <u>Platform</u>).[2]

6. Edit, proofread, and finalize your manuscript (see chapter 14).

7. Hire someone to do the interior design/typesetting and the cover design. This is a worthy investment. People judge a book by its cover, so make it a good one (see the sections in chapters 16 and 17 about designing a cover).

8. Print and publish your book (depending on how you want to publish your book, see chapters 15, 16, or 17).

9. Your personal and professional goals will determine the next steps you take after completing your book (see additional recommendations in chapter 17).

---

2   www.michaelhyatt.com/platform.

Scenario 2: You've Written Your Manuscript

If you've already written your manuscript and realize that it may not be as focused and organized as you had hoped, follow these steps:

1. Create a complete outline for the book *without referring to what you have already written*. If you want to know what to include in your outline, see chapters 7 through 10. In general, the goal is to be able, at a glance, to see where you are going and be satisfied with your destination.

2. Ensure that your outline aligns with your purpose, message, and audience (see chapter 11).

3. Go through your manuscript and plug the content into the appropriate places in your outline.

    • If you find content that is valuable but it's not in your outline and should go somewhere in the book, go back to your outline, figure out where it belongs, and adjust your outline accordingly.

    • If you find content that is valuable but it's not in your outline and should *not* go somewhere in the book, create a separate document and cut and paste the content into that document. You've just started your next book.

4. After doing the previous step, you'll clearly see where you may have more information than what you need or gaps that need to be filled in. Trim down any excess and build out the gaps where needed. This step may take considerable time to complete.

5. Follow steps 5 through 9 from scenario 1 above.

Scenario 3: Writing a Book from Your Talks

If you have audio or video recordings from talks, seminars, or sermons you have done, which contain the content of your book, follow these steps:

1. Transcribe the audio or video. (Transcription resources are widely available on the Internet.)

2. Create a complete outline for the book. If you gave a seminar, you may have already created a speaking outline. Compile all of your outlines into one so you can see the scope of your book at a glance and are satisfied with its purpose and direction. If you want to know what to include in your outline, see chapters 7 through 10.

3. Ensure that your outline aligns with your purpose, message, and audience (see chapter 11).

4. Go through the transcript of each talk and plug the content into the appropriate place in your outline. Rare is the speaker who doesn't take bunny trails, so:

   - If you find content that is valuable but it's not in your outline and should go somewhere in the book, go back to your outline, figure out where it belongs, and adjust your outline accordingly.

   - If you find content that is valuable but it's not in your outline and should *not* go somewhere in the book, create a separate document and cut and paste the content into that document. You've just started another book.

5. After doing the previous step, you'll clearly see where you may have more information than what you need or gaps that need to be filled in. Trim down any excess and build out the gaps where needed.

6. Follow steps 5 through 9 from scenario 1 above.

APPENDIX B

My Writing Timeline

1. I want to have my book in my hands by _____ .

2. I want to be done with my manuscript by _____ .

    (This date should be two to three months before the date in question one.)

3. About how many pages I think my book will be: _____

    (Look at a few books you have on your bookshelf and think about how many pages your book might be based on the content you have to share. Multiply page count by 225 to know about how many words your book will be.)

4. If I write 500 words per sitting, how long will it take to complete my book? _____

    (Divide the number of pages your book will be by 500, or however many words you plan to write each time you sit down to write.)

5. What day(s) and time I plan to write my book: _____

    (Be very specific, for example every Tuesday morning from 5:30–7:30am.)

From Manuscript to Books in Hand

Below is a general timeline to complete your book after you're done writing your manuscript. All of this can be accomplished more quickly if needed. (I've gone from step 1 through step 4 in two weeks with an author, so things can happen fast if necessary.) Or it may take longer if the manuscript requires more than a basic proofread or if the review process takes longer than expected.

1. **Light edit and proofread** (which includes your review of an editor's feedback, second-round changes, and approval) – **two to four weeks**

2. **Cover design** (this can be done while the manuscript is being proofread) – **two weeks**

3. **Interior pagination or typesetting** (which includes your approval of the design and a final review once the book is print-ready) – **two weeks**

4. **Printing and shipping** (uploading files to a printer or print-on-demand service, printing, and shipping to your house) – **two to four weeks**

APPENDIX C

Six-Point Alignment Checklist

If you didn't use a detailed outline to write your book's manuscript, you can use this six-point alignment checklist to see if your manuscript is ready to go to the editor. But first you have to create an outline that represents what you've already written. It's a bit backward, I know, but this will help you to see clearly whether or not your book is well organized.

Follow these steps:

1. Open the document that contains your manuscript. Then create a new, separate word-processing document that you will use to write the outline structure of the book you've written. This outline will enable you to see your entire book at a glance and easily determine how well it is focused and organized.

2. Arrange these two documents side by side on your computer screen so you can see them both at the same time.

3. In your outline document, write down the following sections from your manuscript that show the broad scope of the book, in this order:

   a. Your book title

   b. The subtitle

   c. All the chapter titles

4. In your outline document, write down the following sections from your manuscript that show the specific content of the book, in this order:

   a. Start with your first chapter. If you have any headings within that chapter, write them down in your outline under that chapter title.

   b. If you don't have headings, read through your content and create as many headings as needed to outline the main points of that chapter.

   c. Do this for each of your chapters.

5. Read through chapter 11: Align Your Book and follow the instructions in that chapter to see how well your book is aligned. Make changes as needed to your outline.

6. If you want to make changes to your manuscript based on the new outline you have created, follow the instructions in scenario 2 from Appendix A.

APPENDIX D

Footnote/Endnote Format

One of the biggest headaches you will experience as an author is trying to track down copyright information for quoting or referencing others' resources *after* you've written each chapter. Avoid the pain. Save *days* of work later. Document as you go.

Jane Friedman has a great article on her blog called "When Do You Need to Secure Permissions?"[1] I highly recommend taking a few minutes to read this article. Jane also includes links to other resources if you need to dive deeper into this topic.

Below I have listed the basic information you will need to give proper credit to a source. Consult the Chicago-Style Citation Quick Guide (a free resource) for specific and more detailed examples.[2] Remember, *as* you are doing research or when you run across information you'd like to include in your book, document the following information that will be needed for footnotes or endnotes.

For a Book

1. First Name and Last Name of Author(s)
2. *Title of the book* (italicized)
3. City of publication
4. Publisher name
5. Year of publication
6. Page number in the book where the quote can be found

Sometimes there may be more than one author, an editor, a book with more than one edition or volume, so note that information as well. See the Chicago-Style Citation Quick Guide for a specific description of what is needed.[3]

Examples:

First Name and Last Name of Author, *Title of Book* (City: Publisher Name, Year), page number.

---

1 www.janefriedman.com/2012/01/23/permissions/.
2 www.chicagomanualofstyle.org/tools_citationguide.html.
3 Ibid.

[1] Cindy McGill and David Sluka, *What Your Dreams are Telling You: Unlocking Solutions While You Sleep* (Minneapolis: Chosen Books, 2013), 45.

For a Magazine or Newspaper

1. First Name and Last Name of Author(s)
2. "Title of Article" (in quotation marks)
3. *Name of Magazine or Newspaper* (in italics)
4. Date of publication
5. Page number (for a magazine)

Examples:

First Name and Last Name of Author(s), "Title of Article," *Name of Magazine or Newspaper*, Date of Publication, page number.

[1] Elizabeth E. Winter, "Why it Always Snows on Valentine's Day in Minnesota," *Square Tribune*, February 14, 2011.

[2] Peter Papa, "Eight Gifts to Avoid for Father's Day," *Good Dads Magazine*, June 1996, 55–56.

For Online Sources

Many resources are now online, and sometimes those don't feel as official as a book, magazine, or something you can hold in your hand that was printed with ink. But someone wrote the content, and it's important to give credit … or face a copyright infringement lawsuit.

Sometimes it is only necessary to give credit in the text of your book ("On July 10, 2013, the Target Corporation said on their website that …"). The same is true of a blog entry or comment. It never hurts to include a more formal citation, which in general would include the information below:

1. Author Name(s) of content (if an author is given)
2. Title of article, blog post, web page, etc.
3. Owner of the website or website title
4. Date of publication or date of its last revision
5. URL (the website address)
6. Date you accessed the content (especially if the information may change)

Example:

[1] "Investing in Bangladesh's garment industry," Target Brands, Inc., https://corporate.target.com/discover/article/investing-in-Bangladesh-s-garment-industry, accessed August 12, 2013.

Document Your Resources

Remember to document any resource that you use. Specifics about how to document your notes (footnotes or endnotes) or bibliography, consult the <u>Chicago-Style Citation Quick Guide</u>[1] or search "Chicago Manual of Style endnotes" on the Internet (a number of sites and examples will show).

---

1 <u>www.chicagomanualofstyle.org/tools_citationguide.html</u>.

APPENDIX E

Copyright and Permission Guidelines

According to copyright law, it is illegal for an author to use *any* material that is not theirs unless:

- The material is in public domain and you properly acknowledge the source in your book.

- You use an allowed portion of the material under "fair use" and properly acknowledge the source in your book.

- You receive permission to use the material from the owner of the copyright and properly acknowledge the source in your book.

- The facts or ideas are considered common knowledge—like the earth is round, dates of well-known historical events, mathematical and chemical equations, authors of books, names of movies and actors, etc. (This is general information. But it's still a good idea to document a source if you are uncertain about something.)

- You have direct quotes from an interview that you have personally conducted.

Receiving permission is not an overnight process. In some cases it can take months, especially when corresponding with publishers. Start to secure permissions as soon as you determine you want to include material that requires it.

Most traditional, royalty-based publishers require authors to secure their own permissions. They will have their own guidelines you will need to follow.

Make no assumptions. Confirm your right to copy every resource you plan to use in your book. Take this process seriously and do what you need to do to ensure you are abiding by copyright law and do not delay the publishing of your book.

Below are a few more details and additional resources about public domain, fair use, and permissions. I also include some information about Creative Commons copyright licenses, which are being used more and more frequently on the Internet.

Public Domain

Permission is not required to quote works whose copyright is expired. You are still expected to properly acknowledge the source in your book.

Sometimes authors assume that a work is in the public domain just because it's old, like quoting classic books or hymns. People also make the wrong assumption that because something is accessible online for free it's okay to use. While more and more content is under what is called Creative Commons, Creative Commons does not allow for commercial use of its content, which means you can't sell it. (See below for more about Creative Commons.)

For more information about copyright terms and public domain in the United States, consult this helpful chart from Cornell University.[1]

Fair Use

"Fair use" allows authors to quote a *short* portion of another author's work to support their point. Quoting large portions or quoting excessively is not considered fair. You must also copy the original perfectly, in the intended context, and give proper credit (see Appendix D).

If the purpose of your nonfiction book is to instruct for educational purposes, quotes from other nonfiction sources are likely to be considered fair use. However, if using the quoted material in your book could be considered depriving the copyright owner of income, this is not fair use. Using quoted material from other authors should *help* and *further* their cause, not take anything away from them.

Four common sources that are never considered to be fair use include:

- Song lyrics (and sometimes the title of a song if it is trademarked)
- Short essays
- Poetry
- Online dictionaries or encyclopedias

Using fewer than five hundred verses from one Scripture translation (unless those verses constitute a major portion of your book) is considered fair use for most translations. Every translation requires that you acknowledge the source properly, using the words and format that can be found on the copyright owner's website or at sources like BibleGateway.com, which contains multiple translations in many languages.[2]

See below for sources that I recommend you seek permission for. For more information about fair use, consult resources from Stanford University Libraries and attorney Richard Stim[3] (who also answers many copyright questions on his helpful blog[4]): one on fair use,[5] and the other about four

---

1   www.copyright.cornell.edu/resources/publicdomain.cfm.

2   www.biblegateway.com/versions/.

3   dearrichblog.blogspot.com.

4   Ibid.

5   fairuse.stanford.edu/overview/fair-use/what-is-fair-use/.

<u>factors</u>[6] that measure fair use. Both are very helpful to ensure that the material you want to quote falls within fair-use guidelines.

Permission Required

Securing permission can be a long, stressful process. Sometimes a copyright owner can refuse to grant permission or require a high fee to use the material. If possible, avoid having to seek permission by:

1. Ensuring that what you quote falls within fair-use guidelines.

2. Finding a way to summarize or rewrite the material without quoting or plagiarizing it.

3. Choosing not to use the material at all or using material that does not require permission.

It is best to secure permission for the following situations:

- Anytime you use material from someone you know personally and you are certain will give you permission, even if it falls under fair use. Letting someone know how you are using his or her material can give your book an additional supporter.

- More than a few sentences (fewer than fifty words) from a blog, essay, article from a newspaper or magazine, online resource, etc.

- More than 250 words from a full-length book.

- Personal stories in which people may recognize themselves in your book.

- If another person has contributed to your content in some way and would claim personal ownership of the material.

- Poetry, prayers, and song lyrics. Copyright law is very strict about short works, and you'd be surprised how sensitive publishing companies can be about them. Many authors I work with want to include the lyrics to an inspiration song, poem, or prayer, not realizing that these are protected by copyright law. It's best to consider options 2 or 3 above instead of quoting one of these.

- Scripture, if you include more than 500 verses of any one translation or if those verses are a majority of your book.

- Works of art, images, illustrations, photographs, graphics, maps, charts, tables, images on websites, screenshots, reproduction of advertisements, some trademark

---

6 fairuse.stanford.edu/overview/four-factors.

usage, etc. This is another area that requires sensitively and attention to detail. Just because a graphic is at Google images, that does not mean it's free to use for commercial or non-commercial purposes. Even images you purchase from a stock-photo website have restrictions. Also note that what may be allowed under copyright for print (like a paperback) may be different for an e-book. Be sure to look at the fine print for what is allowed. For anyone considering royalty-free images:

- Check print *and* digital (e-book) rights prices. Sometime they are *very* different—like thousands of dollars different (e-book format being much higher).

- Ask about conveyance of rights, since some companies will not let another party assume ownership of the images. For example, if you buy an image and then a publisher chooses to publish your book, the publisher must also buy the image.

- Beware that finding the cheapest royalty-free images does *not* necessarily mean the best overall deal. Consider all the license terms.

How to Request Permission

If you need to request permission, contact the copyright holders as soon as you know you are going to want to use their material. The process can take a few months, so allow plenty of time for them to respond. Publishers and/or authors usually have specific instructions about how to request permission on their websites or somewhere in the material you are quoting.

Steps to request permission include:

1. Contact the copyright holder. A sample letter is included below. Also see Columbia University Libraries for procedures to secure permissions[1] and model permission forms[2] (you may need to adapt them for your purposes). This website is another helpful resource if you have copyright questions.

2. Request "nonexclusive, royalty-free, world rights in all languages and for all editions in print and other media." This means that the copyright owner can allow others to include the same material in their books that you use in your book. You do not have to pay them a royalty fee; you can sell your book around the world; you can translate the quoted content into other languages; you can create other

---

1   www.copyright.columbia.edu/copyright/permissions/requesting-permission/.
2   www.copyright.columbia.edu/copyright/permissions/requesting-permission/model-forms/.

editions of your book without having to ask for permission again; you can create other forms of the book, like an e-book.

3. Make sure that both you and copyright holder have a copy of the permission letter. Retain your copy in a safe, easy-to-find location.

Sample Permission Letter

An Internet search will provide you with ample examples of letters to write for the specific kind of permission you are seeking. I've included three resources below that give helpful information about permissions and examples you can customize to meet your needs. (I have also included a sample letter of permission at the end of this appendix.)

- University of Virginia Press website, where you can download a Word document of their sample[3]

- A PDF with Permissions FAQs and samples from The Association of American University Presses[4]

- A PDF from Author Services[5]

- A PDF from University of Chicago Press[6]

Recommendation: Make it as easy as possible for the copyright owner to give you the permission you're looking for. If you're working directly with the author, don't force him or her to download a document, print it, sign it, put it in an envelope, go to the post office, buy a stamp, and mail it. Instead do the following:

- Put the text of the request in the body of an e-mail (attach a copy for their records).

- Fill in as much information as you can—like the name, address, and other contact information you may already know—so that even a person on a mobile device can simply fill in any missing details in an e-mail and reply with a yes.

- Make the request warm and professional, but short and to the point. And be sure to extend your extreme gratitude for their consideration of your request.

---

3   www.upress.virginia.edu/information-for-authors/current-authors/ sample-permission-request-and-release-letters/.

4   www.aaupnet.org/images/stories/documents/aauppermfaqs.pdf.

5   www.authorservices.wiley.com/permissions guidelines for authors pdf.pdf.

6   www.press.uchicago.edu/Misc/Chicago/copy_and_perms.pdf.

How to Acknowledge Permission

There are a number of ways to give proper credit to the source of your material.

- A reference in the body of a paragraph in your book
- A footnote or endnote
- A credit line on an illustration, a table, or other images
- On the copyright page
- In an acknowledgments section at the beginning or ending of your book

The best way to acknowledge permission is however the copyright owners wants to receive credit for using their material.

Creative Commons Copyright Licenses

An image like this …

… represents what is called a Creative Commons license. You may have seen one on a website or blog. There are many types of licenses. The license[1] graphic shown above allow you to share (copy, distribute, and transmit) and/or adapt another's content if you:

- Give proper recognition to the source

- Use it for noncommercial purposes (you can't sell it)

- Are willing to share the same content (if you alter it or build on it) under the same agreement.

Creative Commons is "a nonprofit organization that enables the sharing and use of creativity and knowledge through free legal tools." They have "free, easy-to-use copyright licenses [that] provide a simple, standardized way to give the public permission to share and use your creative work—on conditions of your choice. CC licenses let you easily change your copyright terms from the default of 'all rights reserved' to 'some rights reserved.'"[2]

---

1   www.creativecommons.org/licenses/by-nc-sa/3.0/.

2   Creative Commons, About, www.creativecommons.org/about.

Note that "Creative Commons licenses are not an alternative to copyright. They work alongside copyright and enable you to modify your copyright terms to best suit your needs."[3]

Click here for information on types of licenses available.[4]

Creative Commons is leading the way with many content producers on the Internet. If this interests you for your online or book content, you can choose the kind of license you want here and the site will produce an icon you can use with your content.[5] This information is available in many languages.

Permission Release Form Content with Example

If a traditional, royalty-based publisher is publishing your book, they should provide the form you need to submit to gain proper permission. If you are self-publishing, create your own document using the information below. It does not need to be fancy, but it should look professional and include the following:

- Date
- Your full contact information (address, telephone, e-mail)
- The address and contact information of the copyright owner
- A professional greeting and a request for permission to reprint the material. For example, "I am writing to request permission to reprint material from [name of book, magazine, website, blog, etc.]."
- A description of the material you want to use and a copy for them to view. Include:
  - Title of the work
  - Author's name
  - Copyright date
  - Word count
  - Page number(s) if applicable

- Explain where the material will be reprinted. For example, "The material will appear in my book, ..." Then provide the
  - Title
  - Your name
  - Trim size (5.5 x 8.5, 6 x 9, or other size)

---

3 Ibid.

4 www.creativecommons.org/licenses/.

5 www.creativecommons.org/choose/.

- Binding (paperback, hard cover, or other)
- Number of pages in your entire book
- When the book will be released
- How many copies you plan to print initially
- Retail price

- Request permission for nonexclusive, irrevocable, royalty-free, world rights in all languages and for all editions in print and other media. Add, "If you do not hold the copyright or if someone else needs to grant additional permission for me to use the material, please advise."

- Describe how you will give credit in the book. Follow the format described in Appendix D. Ask the copyright holder to provide a different credit line if required or desired.

- Include a place for your name, signature, and date.

- Provide a place for the copyright owner to write and sign his or her name with the date. Include the following words near the signature line: "Your signature affirms that you own the rights to the material outlined above and you grant permission to republish these materials as specified above."

If you want to include content in your book that requires more specific permission (for example, if you have more than one person contribute copyrightable material to your book or you require an information release for content you include in your book), customize the permissions form as needed. A search on the Internet for "book contributor release form" or "information release form for book" will provide other options. Also check out the resources for the Sample Permission Letter above.

If you have a lawyer, you may want to consult him or her to ensure your permission release form is adequate for your needs.

Permission Request Example

Date

Your Name, Street Address, City, State, Zip Code, Telephone, E-mail in block format

Copyright Owner Name, Street Address, City, State, Zip Code in block format

Dear _____,

I am writing to request permission to reprint material from the [book, magazine, website, blog] described below:

Title of work	Author of the content you want to use
Location of the content (website, book, etc.)	Copyright date or date published
Number of words you want to use	Page number(s) if applicable

The material will appear in the [book, study guide] described below:

Title of the book:	Author's name:
Trim size: (5.5 x 8.5, 6 x 9, or other)	Binding: (paperback, hard cover, or other)
Pages: (Number of pages in your entire book)	Release date: (When the book will be released)
First print run: (Number of copies in your first print run)	Retail price:

I am requesting permission for nonexclusive, royalty-free, world rights in all languages and for all editions in print and other media. If you prefer different permission terms or request a fee, please advise. Also, please advise if you do not hold the copyright or if someone else needs to grant additional permission for me to use the material.

Your work will receive the following credit line. Please provide a different credit line if necessary.
        [Include credit line using the proper format from Appendix D].

Thank you for your kind consideration of this permissions request. I look forward to your response.

_____   _____   _____
Name   Signature   Date

Your signature below affirms you grant permission to republish these materials as specified above.

_____   _____   _____
Name of Copyright Owner   Signature   Date

Acknowledgements

I would like to express my sincere thanks and appreciation to the following people who have encouraged me and have played a part in this book being completed:

- Vonnie Dugan. The "monitor" at Bethany Academy who checked to make sure my work was done each day. She also sat next to me regularly to help me with my English.
- My ACT scores. I pursued an English major because my scores in the other areas on the test were so low.
- Tom Heyer, former principal at Bethany Academy, who hired me to substitute and then work as a teacher just out of college.
- Scott Moline and Jesse Hinrichs, who listened to all my "new" crazy ideas, which really weren't new to them, but they were patient with me anyway. And thanks to my other English teacher colleagues: Kathy Schultz, Genelle Clark, Mark King, and David Christianson.
- Ed Silvoso, Rick Heeren, and the Harvest/ITN family. Ed and Rick trusted me to work on their books as I learned PageMaker and stretched my wings in the writing and publishing arena. They never failed to acknowledge or praise my work.
- James Goll. You've been a spiritual father and friend. I've learned more from simply observing your life than from listening to anyone who's tried to teach me something intentionally. I love you and your family.
- Daniel Bymer. Your creativity, work ethic, organization, and leadership have inspired and taught me.
- The many authors who've trusted me to work on their books, including James Goll; Ed Silvoso; Patricia King; Joan Hunter; Joshua Mills; Rick Heeren; Chris DuPré; Brent Lokker; Cindy McGill; Jack Serra; Dick Hochreiter; Duncan Robinson; Audrey Meisner; Kaye Beyer; Alice Patterson; Eric T. Smith; Sean Feucht, Andy Byrd, Rick Pino, Jake Hamilton, Corey Russell, David Fritch, and all the *Culture of Revival* and Burn authors; Mark DuPré; Anthony Hulsebus; Andre Ashby; Steve Ciccarelli; Diane Kukala; Robin Rinke; Jackie Vann; Roxy Lynch; Stan Strickland; Nancy James; Derek Mitchell; Dan and Linda Wilson; and others. I've learned from you and you have become friends. Thank you for entrusting to me what God has given to you.
- Amazing professionals who have provided their expertise and services to my authors: editors and designers Yvonne Parks, Steve Fryer, Ken Vail, Katherine

Lloyd. Editors Nathanael White, Michelle Winger, Kathy Ide, Andy Kauth, Steve Cooper, Danielle Goll, Kristen Alewine. I really enjoy working with you.

- Carol Martinez. You have been a trusted friend in the publishing world.
- My wife, Christina, and my kids, Hope, Becca, Abbie, and Joey. Thank you for your patience and love.
- My parents, David and Ruth Sluka. Thank you for your unequivocal support of whatever I've done (even when I kicked the soccer ball through the front picture window). I've always known you love me.
- My other parents, Bob and Hope Kennedy. You've been loving and wonderfully supportive in-laws. Thank you!
- I will even thank my dog, Raphi, for following me to my office and camping out *under* my chair (he's a very small 3.5 pound Yorkshire Terrier) while I worked. Sorry for almost running you over dozens of times when I moved my chair.
- Facebook friends who provided feedback on the cover and content.
- To friends who have taken time to listen as I process, including Chris Rasmussen, Peter McClung, David Kindervater, Randy Turnacliff, Dan Tripps, Bruce Smith, Robert Douglas, Dave Ihde, Manoj Moorjani, Ken Haase, Jeff Pirk, Jeffrey Thompson, Randy Nibbe, Tiago Bomfim, David Matychuk, Jeff Frick, Scott Cross, Leon Hoover, Nathanael White, John Adams, George Kennedy, Eric Straub, and Erik Stensland.
- My friends and former colleagues at Best Buy. I've never had a better job with better teammates. Without Best Buy, I could not fully provide what I offer my clients today.
- The country and people of Paraguay and the team at Misión Betania. It was a privilege to be with you for 2013. I was able to write most of this book on your beautiful campus and supported by your depth of character and love.

Thanks for believing in me.

About the Author

David Sluka is a writer, speaker, author, and coach who helps leaders prepare, write, and share their expertise and experience in books to expand their influence and multiply their impact. He does this through mentoring and training via services and seminars, creating practical resources, and introducing others to transformational content from respected leaders.

In September 2013 Chosen Books published *What Your Dreams Are Telling You: Unlocking Solutions While You Sleep,* written by Cindy McGill with David Sluka. The book shows you how you can find the solutions you need during the day by just falling asleep at night.

David has had the privilege of working with many wonderful leader-authors, including James Goll, Ed Silvoso, Patricia King, Joan Hunter, Joshua Mills, Chris DuPré, Brent Lokker, Cindy McGill, Duncan Robinson, Audrey Meisner, Kaye Beyer, Alice Patterson, Eric T. Smith, Sean Feucht, Andy Byrd, Rick Pino, Mark DuPré, Jake Hamilton, and hopefully you.

For a full biography, see www.david-sluka.com/biography.

www.write-your-book.com

www.david-sluka.com